CHILD
OF THE
LAND

A personal journey to
change the world
one child at a time

Lee Phillips

ISBN: 978-1-936634-05-7
Library of Congress Number: 2015940134

Cover Design by Denise Kelly

For more information contact:
www.phillipslee.com
email: lee@phillipslee.com

Printed in the United States of America

Dedicated to Zhoe
For teaching me about
strength

DISCLAIMER

I have tried to recreate events, locales and conversations from my memories of them. In order to maintain their anonymity in some instances I have changed the names of individuals and places, I may have changed some identifying characteristics and details such as physical properties, occupations and places of residence.

CONTENTS

PROLOGUE

1997 SINGAPORE - 6 SEPTEMBER

The rapid beating in my chest drowned out sound. I was frantic. In a matter of seconds Zhoe's fingers had slipped from mine. She was gone.

I had arrived in Singapore with my three daughters six months ago. My husband, Miguel, had recently accepted the position of general manager at Stars Restaurant in Singapore. Singapore, the Lion City, is an island of multi-faceted beauties with a population of over two and a half million. Residents from China, Malaysia, India, and more recently, Europe and North America call the island home. The people are like a bouquet of mixed spring flowers. Each individual lily, rose or daffodil contributes its own unique presence and scent. With the influx of diverse cultures, Singaporeans have implemented a system which allows these ethnicities to unite but conserve their individual identity, thus portraying a multi-cultural island that embraced diversity and flourished into an economic power.

It was day 106 as a resident of this tiny country located north of the equator in the South China Sea. I had been enjoying a reprieve from my maternal duties since Tina, the pastry chef at Stars restaurant and Jason the chef took my daughters to see the movie *Hercules*. I was to meet them at Stars Restaurant at six-thirty.

I arrived at Stars and was greeted by three familiar smiling faces. I could identify the girls' dinners by the various stains on their faces. I noticed their milky-white mustaches and knew dessert had been devoured. Sierra, five, was the firecracker in the family. She strutted around giving orders, task-oriented and explosive if interrupted or confronted. Zhoe, also five, represented the calm with an innate wisdom that flowed with the tides and aimed to please. She had a heart that expanded to incorporate the needs of others and a contagious smile. Havana, four, contributed the humor to the clan. The twinkle in her eye showed the mischief being contrived in her little mind. She possessed a quick wit and a free spirit, flitting around enjoying the treasures life offered her. They were beaming with stories about their escapades.

Miguel and I juggled one car between us - a 1981 rust-colored Mitsubishi Colt, that housed a few crawling creatures. I decided to leave the car for Miguel as he usually worked until midnight.

Miguel walked over to say his good-byes. "Lee, the MRT is going to be crammed with commuters going home, take a taxi."

I hugged him. "OK, I'll take a taxi, see you later."

The late evening air was warm. The last traces of daylight vanished as a few twinkling stars filtered into the night skies. We crossed North Bridge Road, to Raffles City where taxis were usually a common sight. The queue for a taxi ran ten people deep. Due to a lull in the appearance of our "Comfort" cabbies I decided to avoid the wait and join the commuters on the subway. At seven-thirty at night the crowds made me nervous. I wanted to keep the three girls attached to me. Sierra and Zhoe curled their hands into mine and I told Havana to grab the hem of my dress. The next stop was a visit to the trusty ticket machine to purchase the various passes with Milo or Kit Kat ads plastered on the front. People occupied every tile in the station. I nervously made my way down the escalator to the platform with my girls.

The train arrived filled with people. I approached the doors trying to figure out how to carve a hole through this block of humans for our quartet. Sierra found a corner, Zhoe slid over to the left. I placed my foot on the train with

Havana's fingers tightly wrapped around the material of my dress. At that moment the doors started to close on my hand. Doors moved before I could open my lips. I yanked Sierra out, but Zhoe was too far over. The automatic doors closed faster than I had time to react. I was forced to release my grasp on her. Panic flashed over me as I saw Zhoe's face flat against the glass, her dark, innocent eyes wide with confusion. Her eyes filled with tears as I pounded on the doors to no avail. Within seconds the train sped away - with my little girl.

The stale breeze from the train blew across my face as my fists flailed in the empty air.

Until tonight, the last time I had witnessed fear in a child's dark eyes, was in Zhaoqing, China in 1993.

CHAPTER 1

1986 – CHICAGO and JACKSONVILLE

The wind whistled as I sat in the passenger seat of the red corvette as it darted through traffic on the highway toward the doctor's office. The bleak winter skies of Chicago deemed appropriate for the heavy disappointment that churned in my stomach.

One second, one incident, one fall, and my future had been hijacked. Dreams, passion, goals all outlined for six months washed away, now wasted ink on paper that would be crumpled and tossed in a trashcan.

I hobbled into the doctor's office in a daze and began the motions of filling out forms and answering questions. The X-ray would confirm my sentence. I sat in the patient cubicle, leg elevated, awaiting my prognosis.

Three hours earlier, Gail and I had a half-hour to practice for our upcoming tennis matches and the Canadian coach was drilling us. He threw up a lob and I turned to move back when I felt the familiar shape of the ball brush my ankle. My momentum made it inevitable, I knew I'd fall. When I hit the court I heard a snap.

Gail and I grew up in Jamaica, continuing a second-generation friendship. Our fathers were born on the same Caribbean island and had played tennis from childhood. I was four years older and our bond began from days in diapers to training on the tennis court. Her family had moved to Ontario in the seventies. She was one of the top junior tennis players in Canada and travelled with the Canadian National Team on the professional women's circuit. I had recently graduated from Jacksonville University and joined the professional tennis tour. We were both playing the Women's Tennis Challenge Series and this was the first of four tournaments. The doorknob clicked and I was back in the doctor's office. My heart raced in fear of the words that would re-define my future. This stranger in a white coat held the answer. He would dispense the information, factually and devoid of emotion and demolish my dream.

His cold, pale fingers wrapped my hand, and he introduced himself.

I forced a polite smile while my body tensed in apprehension.

"You've torn the ligaments in your ankle. I'm going to have to put a cast on."

In defiance and disbelief, I blurted out, "You mean I've got to default my match today?"

"Lee, X-rays don't lie. If you try to walk or worse, play, you'll damage your ankle permanently."

I went numb, my mind blank, too shocked to cry, too frustrated to be angry. I sat for the next two hours watching as layer by layer my leg disappeared under mounds of wrapping. Four weeks in a cast would be followed by four weeks in an ankle brace and then physical therapy.

That evening I sat in the hotel with Gail. "Lee, take this in stride. Once the circuit is finished I'll be back in Toronto and we'll begin training again."

Her Bambi eyes were sincere. Her charcoal Farrah Fawcett shag framed her young bronzed face. Her eyes sparkled with the innocence of a devoted player whose life was passionately consumed with the sport she began at the age of four. *Her* future was promising.

I was the veteran riddled with doubt in my ability to compete at the next level. I had recently recovered after a three month absence because of bursitis in my shoulder. Perhaps my body didn't have the strength to play professionally.

I re-routed my airline ticket from Chicago through Jacksonville to visit Miguel. Miguel and I had graduated from Jacksonville University after playing four years of varsity tennis. Our platonic relationship spanned three and a half of those years.

I remembered our first kiss. During my last semester in college I lived in an apartment across from campus. Miguel had succumbed to corporate America and accepted a job with Del Monte in Jacksonville. One night he came for a visit, like he usually did. His Cuban heritage and chiseled features adorned a six foot one frame, creating an attractive example of the male species. In his buttoned down cotton shirt, red silk tie and gray wool pants, he looked like he was suffocating. He loosened his tie and undid the top two buttons of his shirt, followed me into my room, and flopped down on the bed.

"How's Murphy doing? She was one of my favorite teachers. She made art history interesting."

I looked up from a photograph of Picasso's *Guernica* smiling, "It's the first time in my life that I'm actually enjoying history."

His hazel eyes met mine. For the first time they locked on me without shifting away. He leaned towards me. Our lips touched and he gently pulled me closer.

When I arrived in Jacksonville, Miguel picked me up at the airport and we drove to his parents' house where he was still living. It was a red bricked bungalow with three bedrooms. He and his twin brother had shared bunk beds in one, and his two sisters had the other. Terrazzo flooring lay in the kitchen with a mustard shag carpet in the remainder of the house. His father, Miguel Senior, was an engineer and his mother, Hilda owned a real estate office. Hilda epitomized the Cuban spirit. Her blonde curly hair framed her porcelain face in ringlets and her blue-grey eyes shone with energy. Miguel Senior seemed to carry the troubles of Cuba on his shoulders. His wooden pipe sent tiny wisps of smoke into the air and his quiet demeanor made him fade into the background.

On my second night in Jacksonville Miguel and I drove over the Intracoastal Waterway and headed toward Ocean Avenue. We parked outside the oceanfront Calypso restaurant. A slight chill filtered through the Florida winter night, but the salty air created comfort that transported me back to my island roots. The restaurant's décor featured bright colors and the sound of steel drums added to the ambience.

After dinner, Miguel suggested a walk on the beach. I looked down at my five toes peeking out from the cast like quintuplets.

"We won't go far." Miguel's fingers slipped through mine, and we stepped onto the cool granules. In the winter sky, a few smoky clouds passed over dimming the brightness of the stars.

We walked a few paces listening to the sound of the surf splashing against the sand as it tossed tiny trinkets on shore for tourists to discover tomorrow. I imagined the waves crashing through me and washing my worries away with the receding tides.

Miguel turned to face me, reaching for my other hand. "Lee, will you marry me?"

Marriage hadn't been a discussion even though in my heart I knew we belonged together. His question came unexpectedly, but my response was an instantaneous. "Yes."

The impact of my answer slowly sank in, and when it did it was like an anchor falling to the ocean floor and holding fast. I felt flattered that he wanted to wake up to my face for the rest of his life, but my thoughts shifted to my career. I'd promised myself I'd play professionally for a year and then re-evaluate. But the last few months created a wave of insecurities. Now, I'd be battling another injury and another delay. Faith in myself as an elite athlete was diminishing. I was no longer sure of my ability to compete on a professional circuit.

I entered a tournament three months after my ankle healed. My play was disappointing. I decided to stop competing.

Nine months into my tennis career, I retired.

CHAPTER 2

1987 HONG KONG

In May of 1987, Miguel received a phone call from Larry Nova, who had coached our varsity tennis team in college. He and his wife Joni were now residing in Hong Kong. After working for eighteen months without a break, Larry was calling with a proposal for Miguel.

Larry and his family wanted to go on vacation and offered Miguel and me an all-expenses paid six-week working holiday. The club offered to cover the flights and all our living expenses in exchange for Miguel serving as acting-manager and me teaching tennis.

Our decision to travel to Hong Kong moved up our wedding plans. My parents lived in Shelburne located ninety minutes north of Toronto. We decided to get married there in Shelburne in a small, white stone Catholic church nestled in a field on the outskirts of town.

I asked my grandmother, who sewed my clothes as a child, to please create a wedding dress for me. Her talented hands wove intricate magic into white satin cloth and lace to produce a beautiful gown. I called Gail to pencil in July 3.

My sister Ann, Gail and two dear friends, Lynn and Sandra, along with Miguel's sister Leti agreed to be bridesmaids.

Yellow being my favorite color was chosen for the design of the dresses. The phone rang the minute Lynn got the fabric in her hands.

"Sweetheart, I don't do yellow. You see the pasty color of my skin and my blonde hair. This is mean."

I laughed, "You'll look like a burst of sunshine."

"More like a washed out sunflower. I'm going to have to get cozy with one of those tanning booths to pull this off."

I stood on the stone steps. My life was changing forever.

Ann walked over, kissed me on the cheek and whispered, "It's your time, breathe deeply."

I squeezed her arm, "I'm ready." I hoped. Even though I wanted to spend the rest of my years with Miguel in the back of my mind I recognized my life would be different. I stood under the stone archway and took my first step into a new beginning.

One week later Miguel and I boarded an International Cathay Pacific jet and flew to Hong Kong.

Larry and Joni lived in a four-story apartment building within sight of the country club. The two-bedroom, two-bathroom flat portrayed a mixture of Asian and American décor. An ornate Chinese rug lay on the hard wood floor beneath floral American Heritage couches.

Larry smiled from ear to ear. "Welcome to Hong Kong guys, it's great to see you both."

I pasted on a smile because the little hairs on the back of my neck tingled. During his two years of coaching at Jacksonville University, I had been the captain of the varsity tennis team. During a road trip while pumping gas he asked me to get a receipt for more than the cost of the gas. I refused.

He wore his short black hair parted on the left and was not acquainted with the handle of a brush. His big grin reminded me of the wolf in Little Red Riding Hood. Joni approached and offered a light stiff hug around the shoulders. At least with Joni, the cards faced up and you knew what you were playing with. Larry constantly threw up smoke   screens and juggled a gimmick or two to keep you on your toes. I wondered what Larry had contrived this time.

The American Club consisted of two locations. One was inside the Exchange Tower in Central, downtown, on the northwest side of Hong Kong Island and offered dining facilities to members. The one that Miguel would be overseeing was located on Tai Tam Bay overlooking the Pacific Ocean and offered tennis, squash, massages, gym and three eating areas.

Larry informed me that the money I generated from tennis lessons would go towards paying for the expenses incurred while we were in Hong Kong. That sounded fair so I nodded in agreement.

The summer sun held more heat in the Far East than in Florida. My cotton cap and sunglasses did little to defend against the intense rays. The summer schedule was slow as most of the expatriates flew back to the States for vacation.

Club policy required that membership remain fifty-one percent American, forty-nine percent other nationalities. The club sold debentures that were on the market for US $50,000. They were seen as an investment by American companies like Procter and Gamble and Xerox which purchased the memberships as part of the expat packages offered to their employees. The debentures could be sold for at least what they were bought for.

The general manager, Richard Ross, ran the Central location. He was ex-military and his eye for detail and perfection allowed the Club to operate solidly in the black. His receding gray hair and weathered skin with piercing eyes captured your focus. His wife, Nancy, was easygoing.

Six weeks flew by. I had finished teaching my last lesson and sat in the lounge waiting for Miguel. Jeffrey Ho, the finance director for the club, approached me and handed me an envelope. He was the lone Asian on the executive staff. His eyes generally held a serious look, but on occasion he flashed a smile that accentuated his handsome features.

"Lee, this is your check for the lessons you taught."

I stood and took the envelope. "Larry told me that money from lessons would go toward covering the costs of Miguel's and my stay."

A puzzled look crossed his face. "What expenses? The club paid for your tickets. Larry's apartment is part of his expat package that the Club pays. Your meals were included in the plan. As far as I see, this money is yours."

I opened the envelope and saw a check for the equivalent of $2700 written out to me. I returned the check to Mr. Ho, "I'm a little confused. Larry made it clear that we wouldn't generate income."

"Lee, I'm not sure what arrangements you made with Larry, but I guarantee you this money is going into his pocket. The Club covered all your expenses."

The little hairs on my neck tingled again. "Thanks, I'll talk to Larry, but you need to keep the check."

Once again Larry had worked the system. My stomach churned with bitterness. This time he had used me.

When Larry and Joni returned, Miguel and I stayed with friends while The Club reviewed job options for us. One night Miguel and I were lying in bed and I turned to face him. "I won't consider an offer unless it's worth $100,000." I said.

A smile crossed his face. "Let's be patient. I can't envision a position that would interest us." He was scheduled to have a meeting in Central on Monday.

The next day when we arrived at the Club I looked for Larry. I walked into the lobby and saw him standing at the reception desk.

"Larry, could I speak to you for a few minutes?" I asked.

We walked into the sitting area and I stood so I could look into his eyes. "I want to clarify something. Mr. Ho approached me last week and handed me a check for my lessons. You stated that money earned would go toward our expenses."

His sly eyes looked ahead. "Yep, those monies will cover the cost you incurred."

I held his gaze, "Oh, I was curious as to what those costs were since Mr. Ho said the Club covered the expenses."

I could sense his discomfort as his eyes shifted to the left. "You stayed in our apartment and used utilities."

I enjoyed watching him squirm. "Hey, I wanted to make sure I understood the arrangement." I turned and walked away. He was still a con artist. I stifled my anger.

Miguel arrived back from Central before lunch. The meeting had lasted two hours. "I hope you haven't given much thought to staying," he said. "The offer was humorous. They offered me a job as an *Assistant* to the general manager. Basically I'd be a glorified secretary. Then, you could work under Joni teaching tennis. Estimated salary for us both, $50,000."

I laughed, knowing that housing alone would cost at least $18,000 a year.

Miguel called the general manager and politely declined the offer.

After the experience of a lifetime, we retraced our path across the Pacific Ocean.

CHAPTER 3

1989 – CHINESE CULTURE

Two years later, in March of 1989, Miguel received a phone call from Richard Ross, the general manager of The American Club. Miguel was now working as a sales representative for Procter and Gamble while I coached tennis at the Sawgrass Marriott in Ponte Vedra Beach and designed T-shirts. I had set up a silk-screen workshop in our garage where I created and printed my own designs.

I watched Miguel nodding on the phone. "Yes, OK."

Twenty minutes later he hung up and walked into the living room.

"Mr. Ross, the general manager of the American Club, offered me a job as manager of The American Club on Tai Tam Bay."

"Really! That's fantastic! What happened to Larry and Joni?" I asked and moved to the edge of my seat.

"He fired Larry and Joni because they were controlling too much of the Club. They don't want to hire another husband-wife combination because they feel it'd be a conflict of interest." He looked over at me for a reaction.

"That doesn't bother me. Hong Kong is a Mecca for manufacturing; I'd love to create a line of tennis clothes. It'd give me the perfect opportunity to do research and design. I'm ready to stop coaching. No love lost there."

Miguel looked relieved. "Mr. Ross offered me a salary of $75,000, plus a housing allowance of $1500 a month, all meals covered and two tickets home each year."

"Wow, you got my vote. My suitcase is packed. I get the last laugh with Larry."

Miguel and I embarked on our second trans-Pacific journey with the excitement and anticipation of children pushing the turnstile to Disney World. Like the last time, our first challenge on the "Asian Pearl'" would be surviving the landing of the plane at Hong Kong's Kai Tak Airport! The man-made peninsula runway jutted out into the blue of Kowloon Bay. A true adventure lay before us.

Hong Kong was a paradox of visual complexity, from the jade mountains that emerged at the spine of the island to graceful colonial architecture that divided the skyline, to the sleek glass towers that hovered above Queen's Road in Central. The city was the definition of capitalism, boasting more luxury cars per capita than any other country. Yet its spirit dated back centuries and embraced ancient traditions that have been passed through each generation.

The heartbeat of the city pulsed around the clock, yet time could be taken to admire the precise and gentle strokes of the calligrapher's brush.

Roads were carved into the mountainside. We wound our way to the south side of the island, leaving the concrete jungle behind. Bamboo scaffolding climbed new apartment buildings that rose twenty stories into the sky. We passed the high rise Repulse Bay with its singular architectural statement. It is an aqua blue edifice with a huge peach rimmed square hole in the middle the structure. By western business standards, the hole would represent a significant loss of revenue for aesthetic reasons.

We would later discover the void was designed for the purpose of creating effective Feng Shui, which is based on the ancient Chinese philosophy that promotes harmonious living. Translated, "Feng Shui" literally means "wind and water," the art of balancing opposing forces in life to create a successful, prosperous outcome. The Repulse Bay Condominium was built in front of a mountain which symbolized protection. In order not to trap bad spirits between the building and the mountain, this empty square remained open to ensure a passage for the spirits.

Feng Shui is embedded into many Chinese mind-sets. Decisions are made on the flow of energy and implementing good fortune symbols. The elephant symbolizes wisdom, and the crane longevity. Having these objects in a home promotes desirable living conditions.

We passed the infamous Stanley Market where knockoff designer artifacts from "Chanel" handbags to "Ralph Lauren" jeans could be purchased. Merchandise hung from the ceilings, lay piled on tables. The abundance crowded the stalls.

We turned the corner to Tai Tam Bay, where The American Club stretched along the rugged cliff edge overlooking the bay.

The salmon-colored Club was in contrast to the high rise apartment buildings which looked down on the Club's Mediterranean architecture. The Club's grounds were lavishly landscaped. Red clay tiled steps led up to the doorway into the reception area where we were greeted with forty- foot ceilings. Glass windows opened up onto the view of choppy, aqua waters lashing the coral reefs.

Friends invited us to stay with them until we found our own apartment. I was excited to go house hunting as I thought we could find a nice apartment for $1500 per month. Houses were a rarity and could be found an hour away in the New Territories.

After my first day of looking, I realized two things. One, there was a well-defined expatriate community and they all tended to live in the same areas. Two, apartments were costly and it would be tough to find comparable housing to what we had left in Florida. We were living in a 1,700 square-foot newly built home and paid $850 per month. Two days of looking in the expatriate sections and I couldn't find a single one for our budget. The simplest apartments were renting for $2,000 and the nicer ones for between $5,000 and $10,000.

I asked the real estate agent to look into the Chinese section of town. She drove me along the mountainside, the Honda Accord hugging the corner of the winding turns. Beautiful green foliage cascaded down the side of the hills that surrounded us.

Fifteen minutes later I stared at the largest complex of apartments I had ever seen. I turned around slowly and did it again to let the view settle in. I saw big gray numbers on the top of the concrete structures. The buildings went up to fifty-six. My eyes widened. There was not a blade of grass to be seen. I slowly walked toward building twenty-six and felt a warm breeze cross my face, a familiar scent awakened my sense of smell. I then heard the unmistakable sound of a tugboat horn. My pace quickened and I made my way behind the building where the vast Pacific Ocean greeted me. Plastic containers bobbed in the choppy waters and newspaper pages floated aimlessly by. It was not the aquamarine water of my Caribbean island, but definitely close enough for me. I had found my new home.

I pushed open the glass door and stepped onto a beige-tiled floor. On my left sat a security guard with his head hidden behind a Styrofoam take-out box, his hands busy with chopsticks. The long slurping sounds told me he was eating noodles. He did not even raise his eyes as I walked past. But, I was aware of the others' stares as I waited for the elevator. The Chinese did not try to hide their curiosity. Foreigners were clearly not a common sight here.

I got off on the twenty-third floor and quickly glanced around to count the doors on the floor. Six. My brain could not multiply fast enough to figure how many people resided in this square block of buildings. I knew it was thousands and thousands. The square footage of the available apartment came to 965, but that included the small balcony outside the living room and a portion of the foyer by the elevator. Construction had just been completed.

There were two bathrooms and three tiny bedrooms. The kitchen was the size of my walk-in closet back in Florida. There were no appliances and there were holes in the walls if you wanted to purchase air conditioning units. I walked into the master bedroom, which could probably fit a bed, but the view was magnificent. An expanse of blue water lay before me. A wave of comfort washed over me.

Later, I hurried up the steps of the Club and swung open the teak doors. I looked over at the two young Chinese receptionists, dressed in their navy blue skirts and white blouses and greeted them with a smile. I passed by Jeffrey Ho's office and stuck my head in.

"Hi Jeffrey." I said. He looked up from the stack of papers on his desk and flashed me a polite smile.

Miguel's door was open, and I stepped in and sat on the wooden chair in front of his desk. He was on the phone. He motioned that he was finished. Once he put the phone down, I rambled.

"You've got to see this place. It's basic, very basic, but the view is absolutely breathtaking. The best part is that it fits our budget and we'll be the first tenants. Not to mention that we can purchase it for $150,000! The prices here are ridiculous. There are *no* frills," I laughed. " You know what we could buy for that back home."

He listened patiently, his hazel eyes showing amusement. "I'll go and see it tomorrow. We really need to finalize a contract. Real estate is outrageous here. Purchasing an apartment is crazy, especially with the uncertain future when China regains control in 1997."

The following day, Miguel went to the apartment and was happy with what he saw. He said he would talk with Jeffrey Ho in order for us to submit a contract.

That night I pulled the cotton sheet up to my chin. I closed my eyes when Miguel walked into the bedroom.

"We need to talk before you go to sleep."

I propped the pillow underneath my head and sat up. "Sure, what's up?"

He walked around to my side of the bed and sat down with his arm across my stomach. "I spoke with Jeffrey today. He said that Heng Fa Chuen is known as the local section of town, and we cannot live there."

At first I thought he was joking in order to aggravate me, but the seriousness in his eyes told otherwise. "What do you mean? Is there a law or regulation that prohibits us from living there?"

He shrugged his shoulders. "No. I think Jeffrey thinks that as the manager of The American Club, we should be living amongst the foreigners."

"Is this reverse racism? We can't afford to live where the expatriates live. The apartments that fall within our budget are old and in horrible shape. There's no way that he can dictate to us where to live. Have you talked to Mr. Ross?"

Miguel flashed a look of frustration. He was calm and spoke in his voice of reason. "I don't think I'd bother Mr. Ross with this. However, if you'd like to go and talk to Jeffrey tomorrow that would be your best option."

I had called earlier to make sure that Jeffrey would be in. The summer sun was rising and my cotton pants were sticking to my legs as I walked up the club steps. His small office was simple. The white walls were stark except for a black-framed picture of two panda bears hanging on the wall. He had two stacks of paper neatly placed on the side of his desk leaving enough open space for him to work freely. I took a deep breath before walking through his open door.

"Good morning." I said, trying to sound at ease.

"Hi, Lee. Come on in."

"I wanted to talk with you about Heng Fa Chuen."

Before I could finish my sentence, he interrupted. "Lee, you need to understand the position that you and Miguel are in. He is the manager of this club and that's a title which is highly respected by the employees. If you move to Heng Fa Chuen where the local Chinese live, you will lose face."

I heard the words, but had difficulty digesting his point. "What do you mean by, lose face?"

Like a frustrated teacher who must repeat a work lesson before the students understand the task, he held my gaze. "It means the employees will lose respect for you. They will not hold you in high regard, which could create problems for Miguel when he wants them to follow instructions."

A part of me wanted to burst into laughter, but I stifled my amusement. I told myself to be patient and listen as he tried to explain the Chinese culture. I decided to try reason. "Are you telling me that we cannot live in Heng Fa Chuen because the employees don't approve?"

His eyes didn't move. "You have a stature you must maintain. It's important that Miguel gains respect from the employees so they'll work hard for him."

I was frustrated. "In the western culture you earn respect by the dedication you show to your job and the quality of the work you do. Surely that's more valuable than where you choose to live."

"Lee, I'll make this simple. You cannot live there. Find another apartment."

That sounded like an order. I knew that in the Chinese culture women were seen as secondary citizens, but I was not Chinese. His tone and words pumped the blood through my veins and I knew the heat was rising in my cheeks. My reply was curt.

"If that's the case then I suggest you increase our housing allowance. You're asking me to give up a brand new apartment for one that is riddled with roaches and has moldy walls, but has the correct address." My irritation rose.

"I can't raise the allowance. I suggest you weigh your options carefully as this could affect your future here." He looked down in dismissal and moved papers on his desk. He'd made his point.

I rose slowly and politely said, "Thanks for the input, I appreciate your honesty. I'll talk with Miguel."

In spite of Miguel's advice, I decided to do a little research. I dialed the number to the downtown club and asked for Mr. Ross. His new assistant answered. He put me straight through.

"Lee, my dear, how are you? I hope you're settling in. I've told Miguel that you two must come out to have dinner with Nancy and me in town one night."

His words were spoken with authority, but they were sincere. I immediately became comfortable with him. "I'd love to have dinner; I haven't eaten in Central." I paused. "I'm calling for your input."

"How can I help?"

I shared with him my conversation with Jeffrey. "Am I crossing a line if I choose to pursue living in Heng Fa Chuen?"

I heard a slight hint of amusement as he spoke.

"In time you will understand the nuances of this culture. Material icons are read as the importance of a person. The Chinese will inspect the labels on your clothes, the brand of watch you wear and, most importantly, the car you drive. These are the resumes they look for to evaluate the worthiness of a person. Losing face is equivalent to committing a small crime as it produces shame and is difficult to rectify. I think you and Miguel are a young couple, and your choice of apartments won't make you lose face with the employees. I think your choice of apartments is absolutely fine."

His words calmed me. I now had a better understanding of what I was up against. I spoke with Miguel and told him of both conversations. We decided to move into Heng Fa Chuen.

Miguel and I had arrived in Hong Kong in May 1989. A month later, on June 4, we witnessed the scene in Tiananmen Square, in Beijing when Chinese army tanks threatened Chinese student's demonstrations for democracy. Glued to the television, I watched in disbelief as innocent students fell, as the young and brave fought for what they believed they rightly deserved. Chinese fighting Chinese, it was a culture that I would be immersed in. The more I learned, the more I realized I did not understand the Chinese race.

In Hong Kong, students converged around the Cenotaph in downtown Hong Kong, which in the past had been the center of Remembrance Day to honor soldiers who died in two world wars. But on Bloody Sunday, they gathered to mourn and honor the Chinese students who had died in Beijing.

The Tiananmen massacre shattered the psyche of the Hong Kong people. The 1997 conversion from British to Chinese rule loomed. The concept of One Country Two Systems seemed to dissipate overnight. The theory of the Chinese Government, was that when they regained control in Hong Kong, democracy would continue but, communism in mainland China would remain.

Miguel worked seven days a week from eight in the morning until eight at night. He was in training. His perfectionist mentality insured that he gave 150 percent in everything he did. I decided to follow my dream and research designing a line of ladies tennis clothes. I busied myself making phone calls and traveling into the New Territories in search of manufacturers. The Club was having difficulty hiring a tennis director as pool for tennis pros was minimal on the island. In July Miguel approached me.

"Lee, we really need someone to start a tennis programs. All the kids will return from summer holidays in a few weeks and there will be nothing to offer them. I can promise you the position on a temporary basis as Mr. Ross is still uncomfortable with a husband and wife team working for the club."

"That's fine. I'm enjoying my research, but generating extra income could help pay for tennis clothes samples. I can start whenever you want."

He looked at me and smiled. "Tomorrow."

My temporary position became permanent. Within three months my coaching increased to forty hours a week. The money wasn't bad either. My hourly rate was $35 plus I was earning an annual salary of $12,000. I worked five and a half days, having Saturday afternoon and Sunday off. The weekends were the busiest times at the club which meant Miguel worked on Sundays. I spent my weekends drawing designs and lining up samples and manufacturers.

After collecting numerous samples, I finalized my first line of tennis clothes. I created the brand name "Utopia". The era of neon colors was the fashion. I made a bold statement with neon pink and yellow skirts and tops.

My dream had become a reality.

CHAPTER 4

1990 – CHILDREN

Miguel and I discussed children before we got married. He was eager to begin a family, and he wanted four children. My maternal instincts were still suppressed, as the entrance into motherhood felt like strange territory. I was in awe with the responsibility of raising another human and knew it was a lifetime commitment.

"I'm OK with the idea of four children, but I'd like to give birth to two and adopt two," I told him.

Miguel's thoughts were a little different. "I'll offer you a compromise. If you give birth to four, we can adopt two."

I replied quickly. "You know we're not having six children."

He winked at me.

As I approached my twenty-sixth birthday, I decided that I wanted my childbearing years to be completed by age thirty. Thus the fun began.

The gray February sky that hung over Hong Kong winters slowly made way for the onslaught of a sunnier and humid spring. We experienced a six-week run of clouds with little signs of a reprieve. The dampness consumed our lives. But, I still managed forty hours of tennis coaching in between the showers.

A flicker of hope for a rest danced in the near future: a five-day holiday at the Bluewater, Maribago resort on Cebu in the Philippine Islands.

We arrived on the island of Cebu and were surprised by the friendliness of the people. I realized how much like a chameleon I had become when I had adapted to my Hong Kong world. A year in Hong Kong had wiped away the easygoing manner that had been instilled in me by my island upbringing in Jamaica. I too, had acquired the cold edge that one unconsciously inherits when residing in a big city.

Luckily, the infectious smiles of the locals on Cebu were contagious, and Miguel and I slowly unwound. We took a taxi to the Bluewater Maribago Resort and as we drove were astonished by the poverty that we saw. People lived on the side of the road in makeshift shacks of bamboo lashed together with strips of cloth. There was no running water, no electricity. At night they lit fires outdoors over which they cooked, and used as their source of light. They utilized every part of the chicken-the intestines wrapped around a skewer, which they barbecued, along with the head and feet. But, laughter and song echoed in the air from these humble abodes. These people could not afford to indulge in material items, but their happiness emerged from within. It made me recall the wisdom of the Chinese philosopher, Tao Tzu, "Contentment is wealth."

The Bluewater Maribago was an oasis of luxury contrasting sharply to the squalor outside the grounds. Twelve thatched huts perched on a pearl white sandy beach with turquoise water lapping at the shore, inviting us to enter. I looked forward to relaxing and spending quality time with Miguel.

We had been married for three years. This was our first vacation. We spent the days venturing out to nearby reefs with snorkels and fins. At night, we ate at local restaurants and feasted on lobster, with mangos for dessert. Alone in our tropical habitat, we drifted away into an endless world of sea and sand.

Our five days in paradise allowed us to unwind and gave us the energy to resume our frantic work pace until our next excursion. We planned to visit the United States four months later in July.

Two weeks after our return from vacation I went running with my friend along Repulse Bay and felt unusually tired at the completion of our four-mile route. I had missed my period, but with my sporadic cycle it was not unusual.

I made an appointment to see an English doctor, Dr. Pugh, to be safe and for reassurance. I lay on the examination table while he did an ultrasound.

"Well, little lady, it sure looks like you've got company, you're roughly five weeks pregnant," he said.

I laughed nervously. When I did the calculation, I knew the baby had been conceived on Cebu.

I bypassed the pre-natal classes because Dr. Pugh told me the people who have the easiest deliveries were naïve sixteen-year-old girls. They possessed no preconceived delivery ideas and allowed their bodies to perform naturally. It sounded like a wonderful theory. I'd heard similar stories of women in China who gave birth in the rice paddies then strapped the babies on their backs and continued their day's work. I figured my body was designed to accomplish this miraculous feat, and I'd let it perform as expected. My due date was Christmas Eve.

At my next doctor's visit, I asked, "How long will labor be?"

Dr. Pugh smiled, then paused. "There's no set formula. Females are different. Usually, the first birth is tedious, and you need to be ready to hang in there for a long haul."

"What's a long haul?" That estimate wasn't definitive enough for my brain to file.

He shrugged. "Labor can be anywhere from twelve to twenty hours."

I swallowed hard. *That's* a long haul.

I continued teaching tennis until my seventh month then maintained an exercise program in the swimming pool and played social tennis doubles for another month. In December my parents arrived from Canada to escape the frigid winters and to acquaint themselves with their third grandchild.

On December 23 at 7:15 p.m., we were at a friend's house when my water broke. With my parents in tow, Miguel drove up the winding mountain road to the Adventist Hospital and checked me in. A living, breathing being would be totally dependent on me. I still felt eighteen, doing cartwheels on the beach and dancing until two in the morning. I assumed mothers were grown adults, and I didn't see myself as grown-up. Was I really ready to undertake such a commitment? Too late now! Time had no handle to turn back. Our lives were changing.

My parents found a corner in the waiting room and Miguel followed me into my assigned room. Dr. Pugh arrived and examined me at 10:00 p.m.

"You've dilated two centimeters. You won't be giving birth until at least 6:00 a.m."

"What should I do until then?" I asked.

"Try to sleep."

Sleep? The man obviously had not experienced the pleasure of a contraction, because there was no way I could sleep with my stomach contorting every few minutes. I remembered my sister-in-law, Maria, telling me to stay upright and walk through the contractions, as gravity would aid in a quick delivery. I paced the corridor. I grasped the wall, and let the pain take its toll. By eleven-fifteen the contractions were two minutes apart. I could barely recover before the next one clenched my insides. I stopped a nurse.

"Hey, this pain is pretty intense." I doubled over to ward over the next jolt.

Her wide eyes and unlined face told me she was in her twenties. "I could give you an epidermal."

Miguel leaned against the wall in the hallway and with worried eyes followed each step.

That would mean lying on my back, which did not evoke a pleasant thought. I shook my head and retraced my steps up the corridor. Within fifteen minutes, the pain became unbearable. I found the nurse again. "There must be another option?"

"Why don't you go to the delivery room? I can give you gas. It will ease the pain. I can check to see how dilated you are now."

My sexy hospital gown had its own in-house cooling system that allowed air to circulate around my extremities. Awaiting me in the delivery room was a brown vinyl bed with the inviting steel stirrups at the bottom. I thought, this sterile environment would be the first impression my child would have of our man-made world.

The Asian nurse, with her jet black cropped haircut and starched white uniform, seemed nervous. I slid onto the bed. She pointed for me to insert my heels into the stirrups. All my inhibitions vanished instantaneously as I spread my legs into the V formation and exposed myself to the world. Miguel stood nearby, staying quiet but supportive with a pat on the head or a rub on my arm.

"Oh, dear!" my Asian friend exclaimed, "I see the baby's head! The doctor's not here. The baby can't come yet."

In disbelief, I replied, "I don't have control of this! Surely there's another doctor on staff that you can call."

The nurse's face told me she was panic stricken. She pushed my knees and said, "Close your legs I'll call Dr. Pugh."

My endurance was exhausted. Trying to retain composure, teeth clenched, I blurted out, "Lady, this baby is coming out now! Do whatever it is *you* need to do. I'm not closing my legs."

Miguel watched in awe as the events unfolded; he remained calm. He stayed by my face. I looked up at him. I remembered that he had fainted when he looked in the mirror at the blood after his wisdom teeth were taken out "Keep your eyes on me," I told him. "Don't go looking at the delivery and faint on me."

Sheepishly, he mumbled, "Don't worry, I'm not looking past your kneecaps."

I shut my eyes and tried to let my body take over. Sierra Augustina Solaun arrived at 12:24 a.m. on Christmas Eve 1991. Dr. Pugh walked in five minutes later, disappointed that he missed the delivery. He took his position, looking up at me over my bent legs. "Well, little lady, you mastered birthing quickly."

I caught his twinkling eyes above his green cotton mask and said, "I told you that sometimes knowledge doesn't pay."

The nurse cleaned her tiny body and placed the precious bundle on my chest.

The bond formed between mother and child that first second contact is made is indescribable. An overwhelming responsibility enveloped me. I realized I would help mold this personality, teach and guide her in her formative years, and let her know she could make a difference.

I grew up with specific boundaries between parent and child, too inhibited to discuss topics relating to affection and sex. I wanted to break down those barriers with my children. I wanted them to flop onto my bed in the mornings and cover me with sloppy kisses. I wanted them to embrace all cultures as one. I wanted them to weigh their wealth based on inner peace, not material goods. I wanted them to understand the power of their minds, that each thought can become a reality. I wanted them to love unconditionally. I wanted them to learn the importance of respect and honesty. I wanted laughter to fill their hearts with joy.

I wanted a lot.

The unconditional love that grew between mother and daughter created an indestructible bond that I hoped would last a lifetime. Sierra's dark eyes opened wide with curiosity and at ten months old she was toddling around on missions of discovery.

For her first Christmas, Miguel and I bought her a brightly colored plastic train that she could ride on and push to move. Santa Claus paper flew as my daughter worked for her gift. We pulled the train out of the box. She glanced at it for five seconds and then turned towards the empty box. She spent the remainder of the day playing with that box. She showed no interest in the train for weeks.

I wondered how I could possibly share this love with another child. That question was answered faster than I had imagined. I figured it to be an immaculate conception. Sierra was six months old and unfortunately for Miguel our lovemaking was practically non-existent.

I thought I couldn't be pregnant. But when two months passed with no menstrual cycle, I booked a doctor's appointment.

Dr. Pugh raised his eyebrows when he saw me. "Hi my dear, didn't expect to see you back so quickly."

"I had such fun with those stirrups that I was going through withdrawals."

With the aid of technology, a little gel on the stomach and the movement of a Doppler my internal organs became exposed. With his pen pointing towards the screen he laughed. "Looks like you'll be acquainted with those stirrups again."

I smiled, excited, but nervous. The due date was February 23.

On February 23 the stars hung like Christmas lights strung across the sky accentuating the jet-black night. I lay in my bed with a front row seat watching nature's performance. Stabs of pain began intermittingly in my lower back. At first I ignored the spasms. I began timing them and realized they were arriving at five minutes cycles. Miguel decided not to take risks, and we drove the windy mountain road to the Adventist Hospital.

Dr. Pugh greeted us there, his green hospital pants tucked into his black Wellington boots. "Little lady, I'm going to witness this one."

He examined me. "You're having back labor. I'm going to see if your body will do the work. The baby's torso is where the head needs to be. Hang in there a while and see if we can do this naturally."

My body flinched with each internal tug o' war.

Miguel took his position near my face, holding my hand with his back to my knees.

Dr. Pugh checked my progress. "You have an amazing uterus. It's doing a wonderful job. Keep it up."

Sarcastically, I said, "Great, I'll add that to my resume."

He laughed and resumed his post, reading the newspaper outside my door.

At 11:15 p.m. my body continued its natural course and delivered a healthy baby girl. Havana Marguerite Solaun was born on her due date, with Dr. Pugh beaming. The second she looked into my eyes, her sparkle captured my heart for life. Havana taught me that a mother's love is endless and will expand and embrace all gifts that she is blessed with.

My position as tennis director diminished. I became a full-time mother. I embraced the role because I knew it was the most important vocation a woman is given. The responsibility of raising happy, self-confident children is a challenge I was ready to undertake. The same energy necessary to succeed in business would be important to ensure that our children learned all the right tools for a stable and secure future. If I could instill in them high morals and principles with a strong work ethic success was mine. They in return would teach messages of honesty and happiness to their children and the cycle would continue.

CHAPTER 5

1993 – THE DYING ROOM

When Sierra was a year and a half and Havana was five months old, *The South China Morning Post* published an article titled "Children Condemned to Die" in Chinese orphanages. Children with deteriorating health were left in these rooms to await death. Photographs illustrated the desperation. The vacant eyes reached out to me from the newspaper. The small bony bodies struck a chord in me, triggering a need to help. Somewhere in China a government employee allowed these tiny humans to suffer. What adult could stand by and watch a baby die?

At twenty-nine I was naively idealistic. I could make a difference. I wanted to put an end to this inhumane part of the Chinese culture.

I called the newspaper and was referred to a man named Mick Marshall. He worked with a Christian organization called Youth With a Mission and became involved with several orphanages throughout China.

Mick Marshall was six-foot-one with salt-and-pepper hair. His outstretched hand gave me a firm shake, maintaining eye contact the entire time. He worked out of one cramped room at The Youth with a Mission office.

On his wall, a map of China punctured with colored thumbtacks indicated the locations of the orphanages he had visited. On the opposite wall, photographs of parentless children from the orphanages peered out at me. Mick helped couples adopt children out of China. He carried around pictures of orphans. On the back of each one was a biography. He and I spoke at length how bad the conditions in China were.

Orphanages didn't require workers to be experienced in childcare. Hygiene was minimal. Most children wandered around without underwear or diapers. They would squat over a cement hole or simply relieve themselves where they stood. The orphanages lacked funding and supplies. I asked to join Mick on his next visit, so I could assess the situation and see how best I could contribute.

That summer Miguel and I accompanied Mick and his wife Kay into Zhaoqing China to a small orphanage that was a four-hour ferry ride from Hong Kong. We arranged for the necessary visas and began our journey. We stepped off the ferry at noon in a bustling city of three million people. Motorcycles and luxury cars fought for dominance on the road. Fruit vendors on the street corners showed the signs of budding enterprise. The city was dusty and dry. The smell of stale tofu frying and other Chinese fare filled the air.

We had made reservations at the Chinese Overseas Hotel. We walked into a huge, stark, gray-marble lobby. Three girls in gray skirts and jackets waited to assist us at the reception desk.

Mick's wife spoke a little Mandarin. We registered and were assigned rooms.

The orphanage was within walking distance of the hotel. Bicycle bells jingled through the air punctuating the guttural sounds of the Mandarin being spoken. The concrete buildings stood lifeless, like the pieces on a monopoly board. On the left was a walkway that led to a small office. Mick entered through a doorway of peeling white paint. We crowded in and Mick introduced us to Mrs. Zhang Xia Qiang, the director. A pleasant smile crossed her face as she stood to shake hands. Her charcoal hair was pulled back into a ponytail. Both Mick and his wife had visited this orphanage before. Kay conversed in halting Mandarin with the director. The complex housed elderly people on the first three floors. The orphanage was on the fourth. It was a gray brick building with concrete floors and dark corridors. A somber air surrounded us as we stepped into the building. We walked through the old people's section and were greeted with toothless grins and gestures of welcome.

On the fourth floor we stepped up to a barred gate, which a worker opened from the inside. The stench of urine permeated the air, and six androgynous children looked elated to see us. They all modeled cropped black hair. The children were dressed in a shirt, some wore underwear, and others remained bare-bottomed. As I looked closer, I realized that the children jumping around were girls, and those sitting were handicapped boys.

Miguel and I turned into the first room on my right which was the nursery. Four makeshift cribs consisted of long wooden planks balancing on a steel frame. There were no sheets or covers.

The babies were wrapped in cloth diapers. Thick elastic bands replaced safety pins. The cloth drooped with the weight of urine. A fine red rash covered each baby's skin. The little ones were fed rice cereal through a bottle with a cut off nipple and guzzled it down as the bottle was shoved into their mouths. I touched Miguel's arm. "How are the babies digesting that thick formula?"

He bent toward my ear and whispered. "I don't understand how they aren't choking. They're so tiny."

I was going to find a way to improve this pitiful living.

Leaving the nursery, I entered the main room. Miguel had a video camera and began filming. The large open room was sparse with a Little Tykes slide in the corner and two small weathered tables with chairs pushed up against the wall. A cabinet sat in the middle with a television. A wooden partition separated the sleeping area.

I walked over to Miguel. "This isn't living. How are these kids surviving?"

He put his arm around my shoulder. "They don't know anything different."

The workers were robotic. They were following the black and white writing in an "employee handbook." They were detached from these lonely children. Even the women caring for the babies didn't hold their tiny bodies during feed time.

I turned around slowly. These children were isolated in a cold concrete room all day. Did they ever receive physical or mental stimulation? I wanted to transport them all to a happier place.

Growing up in Jamaica I had seen a lot of poverty, but at least a family unit provided comfort. In this Chinese orphanage I saw abandonment and seclusion. Children devoid of a loving touch.

Two other small rooms were adjacent to the main room. I approached the second room on the left and a chill came over me as I became engrossed in the somber scene before me. The area was dark, damp and windowless, the little light filtering in came from the outer room. In one corner was a hole in the ground, which functioned as their toilet. A hose hung above it with dripping water. Two dark wooden plank beds were placed beside the walls. There were two beds. One bed held a five-year-old boy who lay motionless. On the other was an infant no more than six weeks old. The boy's legs were crossed, his eyes looked empty and hopeless. The baby lay still. A tube ran out of her stomach and her head rested in white milky liquid. I turned to Mick. "Is this the dying room?"

He nodded slowly, acknowledging my fear.

I pointed to the infant. "What will happen to her?" I asked Mick.

"She'll slowly die." His voice had no emotion.

I turned to one of the workers who wandered in behind us, "What's wrong with her?"

"Something wrong with stomach," came the callous reply.

"Mick, couldn't we take her back to Hong Kong and get her medical care? If they've given up on her, surely they'd release her to us."

Mick looked at me with sadness in his eyes. "Lee, you need to come to terms with this culture. You cannot allow the life of one child to jeopardize your desire to help others. I know this might sound harsh, but she's one life. There are thousands more that need our help. They'd never allow us to take her. In their eyes she's another child to bury."

Guilt engulfed me. Surely I could help this suffering child. I asked myself. How could one human detach so easily from another in need? The workers in the orphanage showed no compassion or remorse. The death of a child simply fell into a part of their daily routines. They played their predetermined roles and fulfilled their duties.

I raised my eyes to the heavens and silently questioned the reality of a caring God.

Why should an innocent child be subjected to such pain, sorrow and humiliation? To be left to die with no dignity or love. Are these the chosen few who experience eternal peace longer because they are taken at a young age?

This Chinese attitude was difficult for me to accept. I wanted to cuddle the infant in my arms and allow her last breath to be taken with the warmth and caring of another human. Her listless body lay flat on the hard wooden planks and her eyes were vacant, devoid of emotion. Her arms outstretched above her head with tiny white legs that hung awkwardly from her hips. I wondered what number she was, how many had taken their last breath in this government built coffin. Yes, the dying room was alive in China!

I reached for Miguel's hand and motioned for him to film the dying room.

His eyes darted from the sordid scene back to me. I spoke softly.

"It's horrible. I knew it existed, but to see these lifeless bodies are heartbreaking."

He squeezed my hand. "We'll figure out a way to help. I promise."

The shock of what I witnessed angered me. "It's inhumane. How do the workers stay detached?"

Miguel put the camera down and pulled me closer. "This is a different culture. It's not fair to pass judgment."

The majority of children were girls, ranging in age from infant to ten years old. The few boys in the orphanage were handicapped. In China, a healthy boy carries on the bloodline. Passing on the family name is an honor in the Asian culture. With the implementation of the one-child policy it became important to ensure the bloodline by keeping a healthy son. Long Fei a boy, aged seven, dragged his deformed right foot when he walked. He seemed in desperate need of affection and became Mick's shadow, constantly reaching for his hand. Dajun, eight, sat naked from the waist down. Unable to walk, he simply allowed his eyes to do the exploring.

Two little four-year-old girls, Hanlin and Yafen, locked arms and walked in unison, giggling and laughing. Apart from their shabby clothes and want of a bath, they exuded contentment. Nine-year-old Shuping had cataracts. She attended school and, being one of the oldest, bore responsibilities. She helped preparing the meals and caring for the younger ones. Kwai Ling, ten, played surrogate mother, giving comfort and affection to all the children.

There was an invisible bond that linked these orphans. With no maternal figure around, they looked to each other for love and affection. Near the entrance, a girl sat in a chair with a wooden bar across the front stopping her from getting out of it. She had cerebral palsy and was restricted to that chair; she sat stiffly and only groaning sounds escaped her mouth. To eat, she dipped her head forward into the bowl that sat in front of her, maneuvering her jaws to grab the food. Her eyes came alive with energy and interest when Mick spoke. I could not imagine her lucid mind being trapped in her immobile body. Her stimulation was limited to the odd interaction that occurred when the workers spoke to her or perhaps when one of the children served her food.

When I inquired if there were toys, the director shook her head, "The children too messy we put away."

The workers were not trained in childcare. They accepted an appointed position and remained indefinitely. Their priority was to maintain a simplified routine that did not create an overload of work; it was not designed for the wellbeing of the orphans.

Perhaps my western point of view was materialistic. The smiling faces showed a level of comfort. Was it right to impose my belief on those who seemed content.

My sister Ann owns a Montessori school in Canada. I read a book, *The Absorbent Mind* written by Maria Montessori. One of her best-known principles is the "preparation of the environment."

The author wrote that the period between birth and six years old was the stage when the most important elements of the psyche were being formed. Montessori referred to a child's mind as the "absorbent mind" as it drew from its surroundings. She felt it was important to provide an interesting and attractive environment to entice and challenge children during their formative years.

The orphanage was the furthest thing from a Montessori setting that I could imagine. I looked around this dreary room, where the only color came from the plastic Little Tykes play gym. These children had been dealt a tough hand. How could they possibly develop emotionally or physically? What could they absorb from this cold environment? How could their senses be stimulated? How could they avoid becoming a product of this bleak environment?

Yu Yan, about eighteen months old, sat outside the dying room in a small wooden chair with three attached bars surrounding her and limiting her movement. Her eyes darted around, determined not to focus on whoever was present. She wore a dirty white shirt and sat in her own feces, unaware of the pathetic image she presented. Her dark, fearful eyes did not allow me to enter her world. Unlike the other children, she showed no interest in winning our hearts.

I knelt down in front of her and for a second we made eye contact. "Why is she left in this chair? " I asked the director. "Well!" replied the director adamantly. "She has no muscles in legs, cannot walk."

I thought the diagnosis premature, seeing that the child had not been given the opportunity to try.

This little person who had blocked out the society that claimed her, instantly intrigued me.

1993 June – The Dying Room – Zhaoqing, China

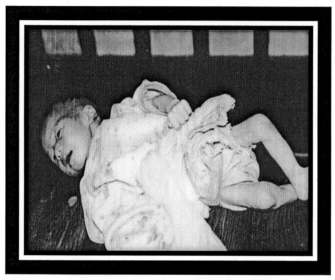

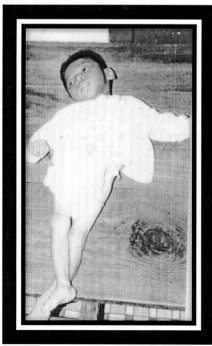

CHAPTER 6

CHILD NUMBER THREE

The images of the orphanage played in a constant slideshow in my mind.

Back in Hong Kong the overabundance of affluence in the city magnified the dire needs of the children in Zhaoqing. The American Club disposed of more food in a day than the orphans ate in a few months.

My mind raced with ideas to raise money for the orphanage in Zhaoqing. Miguel and I decided that we would leave Hong Kong in February of 1994. With the girls now toddlers, we wanted to be close to family. Since it was now July of 1993, I didn't have much time, but I was determined to try and make a difference.

Our family left Hong Kong at the end July for a six-week holiday. My mind kept drifting back to Yu Yan. Her weary eyes and ambivalent nature had pierced my heart. I had a desperate need to discover the person behind those fearful eyes. Sierra was twenty months old and Havana six months. Could I raise another child? Surely I would be able to cope with another daughter. I was healthy and energetic.

I approached Miguel. "Do you think we can try to adopt Yu Yan?"

Miguel remained silent. I could see his rational thought process shifting into high gear. He loved to investigate and research ideas. His decisions resulted from facts, not emotions. He respectfully listened to my wild ideas and gave them ample reflecting and investigation before rejecting or accepting.

"I think we should consider our family dynamics. The girls are still young and need a lot of attention. Give me time to digest this."

I was relieved there wasn't an instant negative. Time, meant hope. I liked the response.

Two weeks after we returned from vacation, I sat at The American Club pool with Sierra and Havana. The girls splashed each other in the shallow end, enjoying a reprieve from the Asian sun. I looked up and saw Miguel walking toward us. He pulled the blue vinyl patio chair beside me and sat down.

"Lee, the strangest thing happened, I was sitting in my office when my mind reflected on Yu Yan. I had this overwhelming desire to try and adopt her."

I reached over and hugged him. "That's all I wanted to hear! I'll go and talk to Mick Marshall and see how to begin the process."

A tingling sensation swept through me. Some way, somehow, we'd succeed in making Yu Yan a part of our family.

I made an appointment to see Mick Marshall who aided in adoptions at Youth with a Mission. At first we exchanged ideas for raising money. An auction would allow us to utilize contacts from The American Club. The club had wealthy and influential members and affiliations that could aid with donations and support.

I then broached the adoption subject nervously, knowing that one needs to be patient with the Chinese government when it comes to adopting.

"Mick, Miguel and I would like to adopt Yu Yan. What are the criteria?"

His thick eyebrows met in the middle as a look of concern crossed his face. He spoke in the same tone. His manner was steady and reassuring.

"Lee, the adoption process is tedious, and there are some initial requirements necessary before the process can begin. First, the couple must be over the age of thirty-five.

Secondly, they must be unable to conceive children. Now, Yu Yan is not an infant and concessions are made for handicapped children. I'm not trying to deter you. I want to warn you that the odds aren't in your favor. You're twenty-nine and have two biological children."

My mind fought the Chinese attitude. How could a government not allow adoption to willing couples? There were literally hundreds of infants dying daily in China. The heat rose to my cheeks. I took a deep breath.

"I'd still like to try. Can you help me?"

He handed me a list of required documents. There were thirty-seven items required of Miguel and me, beginning with birth certificates, police records, bank statements and marriage certificates. A test of perseverance began.

When I left my appointment with Mick, I took the narrow, winding road down to Repulse Bay and reality sank in. Sierra and Havana were small and required a lot of my time Miguel's initial anxieties were valid. Would I be able emotionally to give them all enough time and love? Could I love an adopted child the same way I did our biological children?

I didn't have all the answers, but I felt such conviction to follow my gut. There had been a flicker of engagement when I held Yu Yan's gaze for a millisecond. The connection was powerful. I couldn't explain the invisible bond that instantly linked me to this tiny, abandoned soul, but my heart knew she belonged with me.

In September I accompanied Mick on a trip back to the Zhaoqing orphanage. He was invited to attend a banquet in his honor for a donation Youth With a Mission had made to the orphanage.

The pollution and humidity greeted us when we disembarked from the ferry in China. We checked into the hotel, ate a quick lunch of fried rice, vegetables and noodles, and then found our way to the orphanage.

I was eager to see Yu Yan and arrived to find her in the same position and same chair that I left her in four months earlier. I approached her. When I first knelt down, her vacant eyes dodged mine. Her diaper hung loosely from her waist because the elastic bands had slipped off the cloth. I looked closer and was appalled at the condition of her little torso. The elastic band had cut away at her skin. A two-inch wound on both sides of her hips bled with infection.

I called Mick over. "The cuts look really bad," I told him. "We need to take her to a doctor. I'll pay for the visit." My maternal instincts shot into full gear. "My daughter" needed medical attention and I planned to see that she got it.

The director did not seem bothered by my intrusion. A worker cleaned Yu Yan up and joined me in walking to the hospital.

As we walked through narrow alleyways, heads turned. My five-foot-nine height towered over the people who stood in doorways. Eating from rice bowls, some chattered.

Carrying Yu Yan I walked into the clinic and entered a white room with limestone walls. A woman peered at us from behind a small grilled window. She was handing out appointment times. The floors were concrete with brown wooden chairs strewn haphazardly around the room.

I sat with Yu Yan on my lap, waiting our turn. I wondered if she had ever left her fourth-floor home. She sat in silence, oblivious to the stranger holding her.

We were called in by Dr. Cheung Yuk Yam, a woman in her late forties with thick, black wavy hair that hung on the nape of her neck, her pearl white skin without a blemish. She examined Yu Yan, her gentle hands exploring the injustices done to this innocent child. In the middle of the examination, the doctor pulled her up to standing. Yu Yan stood, not a wobble or a shake.

"The fact that she can stand, does that mean she has the ability to walk?" I asked.

"This little girl's feet and stomach are swollen due to lack of nutrition in her diet. As for walking, all she needs is motivation and an incentive to walk. She has good teeth and eyes. In addition to the cuts on her hips, her thumb is infected probably due to the incessant sucking. She is withdrawn and shows no emotion or reaction to sound. Her hearing could be impaired. That would explain her lack of speech. I will prescribe some medicine that will fight the infections."

The doctor seemed genuinely concerned with Yu Yan's condition and inquired about her background. She was unaware of the orphanage and wanted to know more. We left an hour later armed with packets of white pills.

I asked Mick if it was possible to buy walkers for the orphanage. Yu Yan and the other toddlers would have the opportunity to stimulate their muscles. At least the walkers would allow them mobility. Mick promised to talk with the orphanage director.

That night, Mick and I dressed in simple attire for the YWAM banquet held in his honor. We were taken to a wild game restaurant and informed that it was one of the best restaurants in the city. Inside we were shown to a private banquet room. It's one round table was laden with chopsticks and blue porcelain bowls. The room was paneled in a dark wood with paper lanterns dangling from the ceiling. Five officials, who had been seated, stood and greeted us.

Thoughts of Yu Yan crossed my mind. Her dinner would consist of a bowl of steamed white rice with a few leafy vegetables. The foods being served would help her nutritionally deprived body. The nutritionally inadequacy and scarcity of food in the orphanage contrasted with the abundant display in the restaurant was difficult to digest.

The first dish arrived, a true Chinese delicacy: shark fin soup – shredded shark in an unappetizing murky brown broth. This was the beginning of an eclectic array of foods.

The ivory teeth of the officials were in full view as they beamed at the dishes that followed. A huge bowl of shrimp was placed on the table. I spooned myself a large helping and methodically shelled them, thus taking up time and allowing other dishes to slide by.

Mick was an honorable guest and sampled all the dishes, including, frog, rabbit, eel, duck, pig stomach and the finale, dog. I winced as I saw Mick delicately place his chopsticks around the dark meat and put it into his mouth. He looked across at me and winked, "Just like beef stew."

At the hotel I lay on my bed with a full stomach. I wondered if Yu Yan even knew how that felt. The injustices of life are disturbing. Why one child is born into hardship and another into comfort, cannot be answered. I hoped I could change the fate of Yu Yan.

CHAPTER 7

1993 OCTOBER - PROGRESS

On my return to Hong Kong, Miguel and I began the first phase of the adoption process. We had to gather original documents, get them notarized and then authenticated by the country in which the forms originated. My birth certificate from Jamaica, his from New York along with our marriage certificate from Canada and the list continued.

We had decided to leave Hong Kong permanently and hoped to take Yu Yan with us. We had five months to complete the adoption.

I made my next visit to the orphanage in October. My friend Jennifer accompanied me.

Jennifer and I arrived in Zhaoqing to the familiar aroma of Chinese vegetables sizzling in a wok. Thick brown smog hung over the city. I recognized one of the cab drivers from a previous visit and pushed my way through the crowd, waving toward his car. We checked in at the hotel, washed the city's dirt from our faces and headed to the orphanage.

The children welcomed us with shiny white smiles, taking our hands and leading us into their world. By now, the director felt comfortable with my visits and waved us on. There were new faces in the nursery, and a couple old ones were gone. I never had the heart to inquire why the babies disappeared. The answer I would get was that they had been adopted, but I knew that to be improbable.

No matter how many times I visited the fourth floor, the pungent stench of urine caught me off guard. Two metal walkers added to the furnishings in the main room; Yu Yan and another toddler sat comfortably in their moving chairs. The circular stainless steel bars had small cloth seats with two holes that allowed the children's legs to touch the ground. The wheels on the bottom allowed them to push off and move around. The workers pointed to them with broad smiles of pride. Yu Yan's cuts had healed remarkably well. She seemed to be getting exercise from her allotted time in the walker.

I planned on taking Yu Yan for a physical evaluation and having her tested for hepatitis which was rampant in China. Hepatitis is a liver disease caused by a virus.

Mick had relayed a story to me about an orphan called Mai Ling, Ten years old, had jet black hair that fell to her shoulders and big black eyes yearning for love, Mai Ling had been born without a right arm. Two years earlier a woman from Boston had been approved to adopt her. The woman corresponded with the girl who became aware of the pending adoption.

The prospective mother arrived to collect Mai Ling but was appalled by the conditions in the orphanage. She departed for Boston alone the next day, shattering Mai Ling's hopes. After a month of re-considering her actions, the woman resumed communication with the orphanage, apologized for her actions and decided to continue with the adoption. She returned and took Mai Ling for a medical exam where she discovered that Mai Ling had contracted hepatitis. She panicked and said that she could not take a child with this disease. Mai Ling was abandoned once again.

I heard through the Chinese adoptive-parent grapevine that a family became aware of Mai Ling's plight and began the process of trying to give her a home.

Hepatitis is a condition that needs a lot of attention and I wanted to know what I was dealing with in regards to Yu Yan's health. The diagnosis would not deter my decision, but it would give me time to plan for any necessary medical treatment.

Next to the hotel was a Chinese travel agency that provided translators for a fee. I called to hire one to accompany me to the hospital. Peng Jianlan was appointed to me for the day. She was twenty-two, with small pixyish features and a pair of oval eye-glasses that rested on the bridge of her nose. She apologized for her broken English, while I replied that my Mandarin was non-existent. She asked to be called Erin.

I briefed Erin on my intention to adopt Yu Yan and said that I had not informed the orphanage because I had to be certain that I qualified. I collected Yu Yan and joined by a worker headed to the clinic. We maneuvered our way through the maze of alleys and trekked the one mile to the white limestone building. Dr. Cheung was on duty and I requested to see her again. She was pleased with Yu Yan's progress and inquired if she was walking. I explained that I was in the process of adopting Yu Yan. In the midst of our conversation an idea struck me.

"Erin, would you please ask the doctor if she would be willing to go to the orphanage a few times a week and work with Yu Yan to help her walk? I will pay her."

Erin showed discomfort. I guessed it to be in regards to the fact that offering payment might be illegal. But she went ahead and translated my request. The doctor's eyes darted around the room and then pointed for us to go outside.

"Yes, I'll help the girl," the doctor said. " But no one is to know that I'm doing this."

I looked at Erin. "I will tell the director that the doctor is volunteering her time. Please, tell her that I will pay her four hundred yuan. (equivalent to fifty dollars)"

The doctor continued with the test and checked for AIDS and hepatitis.

The nurse tried to locate a vein in Yu Yan's pure white arm. It was a long task and when   accomplished, the big tears rolled down Yu Yan's cheeks. It was the first time I had seen a crack in in the little girl's stoic facade. I requested a written diagnosis of Yu Yan's condition. Both test results came back negative.

When the doctor was finished, she turned to Erin. "Can I walk with you to the orphanage?"

She collected her medical bag, hung her white coat on a silver hook and then went out a back door to collect her bicycle. She walked the bicycle alongside us, obviously intrigued by this "guylo" showing interest in a Chinese orphan.

Upon our return to the orphanage Erin spoke to the director in regards to why the doctor was with us. The administration accepted the situation nonchalantly.

We walked Erin back to the travel agency and paid the equivalent of $25 for her services. After I paid the bill, she pulled me aside.

"You, special. You have big heart. Next time you need help, you call and ask for me. I work with you for no charge."

A warmth swept through me. I blushed. I extended my thanks again and promised to call her on my next visit. Her words touched me. The heavens were watching, placing Erin in my life. The signs kept emerging along my journey, confirming that I was on the right path. But I knew it would take faith and determination to make this quest a reality.

Jenny and I spent the next day filling buckets with water and soap so that we could bathe all the children. There were no showers or tubs on the floor. I assumed the older children simply wiped up to the best of their ability under the small tap that hung over their toilet, the hole in the floor. I had no idea how the younger children stayed clean.

I approached the older girl with cerebral palsy who was trapped in her wooden chair. I thought she would enjoy the scent of the soap and refreshing water on her skin. I stepped in front of her and removed her shirt. Her face contorted with anxiety and she let out a high pitched scream. I backed off quickly. One of the workers ran out waving her arms. Suddenly, I realized "she" was actually a boy. With hand signs I tried to apologize. He regained his composure and managed a crooked smile. I did not try to bathe him.

The scene did not go much better with Yu Yan. She shrieked when her toes touched the water until I wrapped her with a towel. I covered her with lotion and powder. A fresh floral scent filtered through the rooms.

Jenny and I caught the noon ferry south. Leaving Yu Yan behind became more difficult with each visit. I now felt responsible for this tiny child. Her eyes showed no recognition when I picked her up, but she had captured my heart.

CHAPTER 8

SUPPORT

Late October breezes tempered Hong Kong's heat. Miguel and I were eating a pleasant lunch at The American Club and discussing the possibility of sponsoring an auction to raise money for the Chinese orphanages. A friend, Kathy Goossen, walked over and pulled a chair to our table. She was involved with the social activities of the expat community, and I passed the idea by her.

"An auction takes a lot of planning." Kathy said. "The plight of the children in China is riveting, but you'll still need to entice people. There's a lot of disposable income in Hong Kong, and people will bid freely if they're really intrigued."

I was too focused on the idea to consider other options.

"We've made a lot of contacts in our five years here and I think we can call in favors." I replied.

Kathy had been to a few auctions and gave constructive suggestion into the organization and prizes. With a big grin she said, "My husband, Marty, has run these fund raisers before. I'm sure I could coerce him to volunteer his time."

Marty was an outgoing fun person and the thought of him in charge was appealing. "Thanks Kathy. That would be fantastic."

My next phase was to plan the auction. I worked with Mick from Youth With a Mission and identified five orphanages that were close enough for us to help fund. I decided, the best idea was to itemize the needs of each orphanage in such a way that people would see where the dollars raised were spent. We wanted the money to purchase cribs, beds, comforters, clothes, rice cookers and have enough to allow us to repaint the Zhaoqing orphanage. We were a little worried. It was now October 1993. The auction was scheduled for January 21, 1994.

Miguel put in overtime by calling in favors from suppliers and contacts. His calm demeanor and subtle charisma drew people to him. Whenever he embraced an idea, he became consumed by it, which created the driving force behind the effectiveness in acquiring exciting and exotic donations. He called the florist that provided flowers for the club and they agreed to donate a centerpiece for each table.

Mick at Youth With a Mission informed Miguel and me that two factions in China were fighting for the power to rule on adoptions. One was the Ministry of Justice and the other was the Civil Affairs Department. The Ministry of Justice favored delegating the responsibility for overseeing adoptions to designated "Adoptive Agencies" as it legitimized the process. The Civil Affairs Department preferred individuals pursuing adoptions, as that would not be perceived as "child selling." A moratorium on international adoption was in place and all dossiers were put on hold. Nothing was being approved until a decision was finalized.

Miguel and I were eating dinner at the club coffee shop discussing Mick's phone conversation.

He took a sip from his diet coke. "If the Ministry of Justice wins the battle it would really delay our adoption."

The waiter was placing our plates in front of us when I replied. "Let's hope the Civil Affairs gains the power because we are not represented by an agency."

Miguel picked up his fork. " Sounds like the infamous Chinese 'waiting game' is in effect. This could put the adoption back, a week, a month, even a year."

I bit into my pita sandwich. My frustration was rising.

"We need to remain positive and continue what we're doing." Miguel said.

In the meantime, he and I scrambled to retrieve documents from all corners of the world.

I scheduled a "home study". It was an in-depth review of the adoptive parent's background requested by the Chinese government. The interview was conducted by a certified social worker to evaluate the adoptive parent's relationship, parenting ideas, medical history, employment verification plus their financial status and criminal background check.

An adverse report could disqualify us from adopting. Although usually only a criminal record or poor financial status could preclude the parents. The intent was to create a good match between the child's need and family's ability to meet those needs.

Mick's wife Kay was a certified social worker and would conduct the grueling five-hour interview. First she would talk to each of us individually and then she would interview as a couple. She'd dissect our lives from childhood on and even discuss Miguel's and I's sex life. Our whole life would be placed in the hands of Chinese officials. They would determine our worthiness as a parent to a child who has been malnourished and living in deplorable conditions.

The next morning Miguel kissed me on my forehead before leaving for work.

"Have fun today," he said. "My interrogation was long. Don't you be impatient. I know how defensive you are. Be on your best behavior." He smiled as he spoke.

Kay entered our tiny apartment. She stepped into the living room that boasted two floral couches from the States. She sat on the loveseat and I sat opposite her on the couch that filled the entire wall of our matchbox home. Kay opened her briefcase and pulled out a stack of papers, which she placed on her lap. Her plump, rosy cheeks and good-ole-gal country smile put me at ease.

The first pages of questions were standard information. My birthplace, family background and childhood tales. Kay then paused, and her green eyes held mine, stating without words that the next question would be tough.

"Lee, how will you cope with a handicapped child in your life? Are you ready to make the sacrifices necessary to incorporate her into your family?"

The word "handicapped" startled me like a spark that darts from the burning logs in a bonfire and catches you unaware. Even though I was utilizing the medical diagnosis that she was handicapped to help enable the adoption, I never thought Yu Yan to be a *special needs* child. I sat in silence as my facts untangled, and grasped the concept of what she had asked.

"Kay, I truly believe that with medical attention, physical therapy and a stimulating environment, Yu Yan will thrive."

She slid her pen onto the paper and looked intently at me. "You need to go into this adoption process with the knowledge that you may have a special needs child. The medical reports states she has congenital cerebral delayed development with a small head deformity and mental retardation and that there is evidence of mild malnutrition, possible deafness and at twenty-six months she is barely walking."

Her cold delivery set my defensive mechanisms into motion. I possessed no medical research, no degree in psychology, and no training in childcare. I based my unprofessional diagnosis on simple observation. I had an innate maternal gut instinct about this little girl who visually connected with me for a millisecond in a dingy orphanage room in the middle of China. I knew she could blossom into a healthy and beautiful being, although, I knew no judge in America would allow such a prognosis as evidence in a courtroom.

They say love is blind. Once it's a reality, there's no deterrent, no turning back. You are consumed by a passion that creates a belligerence that you use to protect the one you love. Yu Yan consumed my heart and I was blinded.

With verbal sword in hand, I inhaled and exhaled deeply and prepared to defend myself against the writings of Chinese bureaucrats who labeled this orphan child an invalid.

"I know I sound naïve, but I'm confident in Yu Yan's ability to gain strength once her environment changes. If she does have a form of retardation, then yes, I'm willing to do whatever it takes to help her."

"What if you go on a family ski trip? She can barely walk. How would you handle the situation?"

I recalled skiing once. I was fifteen and attending boarding school in Canada. That day, I spent the entire day bumping down the slopes on my rear end. After that attempt, I crossed skiing off my lifetime itinerary, along with a promise to avoid frigid temperatures at all costs as my island blood rebelled when the thermostat dropped below eighty degrees.

"I'm not a skiing fan, but I'd let Miguel take the other two girls up the hills and I'd stay with Yu Yan in the chalet drinking hot chocolate and playing games."

Kay shifted and went on. "I want you to be aware of the changes that can occur when you have a handicapped child. It could put a lot of strain on your marriage and limit the time you spend with your biological children."

"Life's full of challenges. Whether it's with Sierra, Havana or Yu Yan I'll have to address each one as they occur. Yu Yan belongs with us; I know it in my heart. I want to offer her a life filled with warmth and love. She deserves that chance, and we can give it to her. I know she'll have lots of questions and insecurities as she grows, but the other girls will too. I'm ready to face whatever physical, mental and emotional problems that come with our decision."

Kay's fingers danced on the page as she jotted down her notes. "It's my duty to magnify issues that I foresee developing. You're committing to a lifetime responsibility. You need to be aware of the obstacles that may arise."

Maybe I was stubborn, maybe even flirting with denial, but I trusted my gut and no one at this juncture could dissuade me from my commitment to Yu Yan.

After Kay filled in pages of forms, my throat was dry from all the talk. When she packed all her papers in a folder and stood, she said, "Thank you for your time. I will submit my report and file them in the next few days. Good luck."

"Thanks for your help." I replied and closed the door behind her.

Miguel and I were notified that once all our documents were notarized, the whole package needed to be "chopped" with a red Chinese seal that authenticates paperwork. It had to be applied by a Chinese embassy and couldn't be done in Hong Kong. Los Angeles was the closest embassy. Either we fly to Los Angeles, or find someone who could deliver the documents for us. Obstacles continued to block our way, but we were determined to knock each one down as they arose.

We were put in contact with Mrs. Liu Nam Zheng, who was in charge of the Civil Affairs Department in Beijing. She gave the final approval on adoptions. Miguel asked one of the Club's employees, Gary Mak, who spoke Mandarin, if he would help us communicate via telephone with Mrs. Zheng. I sat, watching the interaction of Miguel articulating each word to Gary and then Gary in his guttural Mandarin accent pass the message onto the mainland. I imagined a lady sitting behind a desk with a pile of papers in front of her. She controlled Yu Yan's fate. She will sift through each page of the adoption application and analyze the worthiness of two strangers' ability to care for an unwanted infant. Our intent with the phone call was to know the probability of approval and, the possibility of the adoption being completed by our February departure date.

Gary replaced the receiver and translated the remainder of the conversation.

"Since the child is classified as handicapped, the approval is assured. If all the documents are completed and the moratorium lifted, the adoption should move quickly."

The news was encouraging, but Miguel and I remained apprehensive due to the internal conflict between the Civil Affairs Department and the Ministry of Justice, knowing that the Chinese government was infamous for long delays.

November arrived and Miguel and I were immersed in organizing the auction packets to mail out to perspective sponsors. We made phone calls; we wrote a cover letter explaining our goals for the orphanages and enclosed photographs showing the poor conditions in Chinese facilities.

My friend, Cindy, who was helping me with the auction, joined me on my fourth visit into Zhaoqing. On the ferry over we looked like two noodles in a rice bowl as we were the only non-Asians aboard. Our towering frames and sharp features created curious glances from the Chinese passengers.

Cindy was unable to bear children due to a condition with diabetes and was in the middle of adopting a Chinese child. She had already gathered all her documentation and was close to submitting her adoption paperwork. Cindy and her husband qualified under the new policies for adoption. They were unable to have children and were over the age of thirty-five. Living in Hong Kong had opened up their options more quickly than living in the United States where the demand for babies was higher than availability. In China, foreign couples were guaranteed a baby once all documentation had been submitted.

Women in China had been considered second-class citizens. They were to be kept indoors or within the boundaries of their courtyard.

Foot-binding became a status symbol of the wealthy but spread throughout China except for the peasants on the farms who relied on women for labor. When girls were seven, wet strips of cloth were tightly wrapped around their feet, bending all their toes except the largest one under the sole of each foot. A makeshift wooden sole was placed under their heel which allowed them to walk stiff legged, like little robots. Once the deformity became permanent, a woman still had to keep the bindings on, just so she could walk. Petite feet were considered beautiful. It wasn't until 1949 that this practice ended.

Most changes came during The Cultural Revolution (1966-1976) which was mandated by Communist Party Chairman Mao Zedong. He ordered that the Communist Party must be cleansed. He waged a war against the "traditionalists" who revered ancient Chinese ways and intellectuals, artists, writers and professors - anyone whose independent thinking suggested sympathy for capitalism. He gave power to the students who joined the Red Guards and went on rampages in the cities, torturing any who deemed to be pro-capitalism.

Children were encouraged to inform on their parents and friends. No one could be trusted. During this period, there was no regard for population control as Mao believed a huge population provided protection against aggression.

Mao died in 1976 and the nation felt that their shackles had been opened. Deng Xiaoping emerged as the next leader and introduced the New Family Policy, which officially restricted each family to two children, who were to be conceived four years apart. Family planning was controlled collectively within each community. Villagers were aware of whose turn it was to give birth. If someone got pregnant out of turn, there was immense peer pressure to have an abortion.

Due to the huge number of uncontrollable births during the Cultural Revolution, there was a large new generation of child-bearing age. It became obvious that more stringent laws had to be enforced. The single-child policy was introduced in 1979.

This policy operated on militant philosophy. Each factory, office, or institution was in charge of controlling births. To ensure enforcement, threats were made that all workers (not only an offender) would forego their bonuses if a second child was born. To make the policy more attractive, other incentives were offered such as bigger houses, free medical care and guaranteed child-care facilities. If someone gave birth to a second child, they were fined.

The mother-in–law was usually the persuading voice to give a girl up for adoption or abandon her in order to try and give birth to a boy. There were stories of female infanticide in a few of the provinces where the ratio between boys and girls were almost two to one. The evidence was even more blatant in the overcrowded orphanages, where ninety percent are girls. The other ten percent are handicapped boys. A handicapped child is seen as bad luck and cannot carry the bloodline.

With over twenty million births a year in China, the government became desperate to restrict population growth due to fear of mass starvation in the future. The harsh repercussions of this law became obvious as families disposed of their girls since they could not carry on the bloodline. Their desperate need to have a male child drove families to abandoning baby girls or killing them. An unforeseen adoption market opened up rapidly as the female population in orphanages boomed and outside agencies became aware of the abundant available female babies.

The ferry docked. I was now at ease with this Chinese town. The orphanage had become a magnet for me. My need to help these forgotten children was a permanent daily thought rolling through my mind. My monthly jaunts allowed me to offer a little comfort to their world.

I located a taxi and we headed for the Overseas Hotel. Once we checked in, I called Erin to see if she was available. She arrived within the hour. I'd brought her a sweater and chocolates, which she accepted with a big smile.

"I don't have to work today. I can stay at the orphanage for as long as you need me," Erin explained.

This was Cindy's first visit to a Chinese orphanage. She had purchased winter clothing for the children, as the cold weather from the north would be whistling through the stark rooms. Whatever emotions churned inside her I could not read them on her face when she stepped through the steel gate. She instantly assessed the situation and greeted the children warmly with smiles and hugs. She then handed out her gifts.

The room was damp and cold. There was no heat in the orphanage. The children kept warm by layering all their clothes onto their frail bodies. Their wardrobe was limited. The stains on their shirts advertised their previous meals. We could smell the stale, bitter stench of the children who had accidents in their pants. Cindy's purchases were a welcome sight, and the children's eyes widened with excitement.

The scene in the orphanage made one realize the importance of how simple pleasures can affect children. Their faces exuded happiness. Their needs were basic; they did not look at the label on a shirt, they valued clothes that would insulate them from cold air. They did not need name brand shoes; canvas slip-ons would suffice; one special teddy bear or doll would be a dream come true. Beyond basic material items, what they needed was a warm hug and someone to look them in their eyes and tell them they were loved.

These children lived on the fourth floor of a concrete block building. If they were tall enough to peep through the bars on the window, their view was of more concrete buildings. Trees, flowers and grass were not a daily sight for them; fresh air was a luxury. Nature's gifts like sunlight on one's body, fresh air filling one's lungs, the scent of jasmine flowers - were denied them.

How many times when you walk the beach do you allow the grains of sand to filter between your toes or notice the multitude of unique shells that the ocean waves have tossed on shore? How often do you stop and listen as the breeze whistles through the trees, or feel the cooling touch of the rain? Unfortunately, at times people neglect to appreciate the beauty that surrounds them.

The orphans in Zhaoqing would never be given the chance to experience those wonders.

Yu Yan was in her little walker. I took her out and dressed her in a pair of red sweatpants and a green sweatshirt embroidered with an elephant. Her right thumb rested in her mouth and her hair boasted a typical bowl cut. Her feet were bare and felt like ice. She stood motionless. She did not move a toe.

Dr. Cheung arrived when I was still studying Yu Yan in her frozen pose. The doctor smiled as she greeted me and pulled out a small brown paper bag and a colored notebook in which she had been logging Yu Yan's progress. I checked with the director and it appeared that over the past month the doctor had visited at least once a day during the week.

The doctor reached into the bag and put a few golden raisins in her palm. She stood ten feet away from Yu Yan and motioned for her to move forward. I could see the recognition in Yu Yan's eyes as they opened wide at the sight of the raisins. With much care and effort, she shuffled her tiny feet forward with the precision of a tightrope walker. Her legs were unsteady, but she moved until she was able to claim her reward. She delicately picked up one raisin and placed it in her mouth, chewing slowly, savoring the texture and sweetness of the dried fruit. She repeated the routine until all the raisins had been consumed.

Once the task was complete, Yu Yan inserted her thumb back into her mouth and remained perfectly still. It seemed as if her feet were rooted to the small green tiles. Eventually I scooped her up. Her legs quickly wrapped around my waist and I returned her to her chair with wheels. I was pleased with her progress and felt confident that she would be running around within a few months.

My mind re-wound back to my initial conversation with the director. I thought how Yu Yan might have been be confined to a chair for a lifetime had a little attention not been given to her. The orphanage decided to dictate her fate, as it had for many that preceded her and the many more that would surely follow. I knew that I could not change the lives of all these children, but adopting Yu Yan was a small beginning.

The doctor asked for Cindy and me to follow her back to her apartment. That was an unusual request. In my four years of living in Hong Kong, being invited into a Chinese person's home was rare. Entertaining occurred at a restaurant.

I turned to Erin. "Thank you so much for your help."

A pretty smiled crossed her face. "Anytime. You call me anytime."

We walked side by side as the doctor held onto her silver bicycle. The hawkers were firing up their woks, and the aroma of ginger and fish sauce filled the air. The concrete block buildings, stark and bare displayed no apparent color on the outside, No curtains framed the windows or painted signs invited us in. The stores we passed sold the essentials: blankets, straw mats and toiletries. Their simple interiors had enough furniture to display the items and a wooden chair for the clerk.

When we arrived at the doctor's home, she chained her bicycle to a rack downstairs and we climbed two flights of stairs to her apartment, conversing with smiling gestures and nods. We entered the door into a living room furnished with a wooden two-seater couch, and a matching single chair to the left. The doctor pointed to a TV, her face beaming. A TV was a luxury item in mainland China. Cindy and I sat on the couch while the doctor took the single seat.

A Chinese man entered the room. His thick, jet-black hair was parted on the left and his welcoming smile showed glimmering white teeth. Cindy and I stood and shook his hand. He was the doctor's husband. A pencil and paper rested on small table. The doctor's husband sat and wrote, saying that he was able to write English but could not speak it. Notes were jotted down and passed back and forth. His wife wanted the exchange of money to be done privately. I handed her an envelope that contained the equivalent of fifty dollars and asked if she would please continue to visit Yu Yan. She agreed.

The next day, a Sunday, we decided to take the children out for a picnic. We dressed six girls and one boy and found shoes to fit them.

Two of the workers joined us. One of them, I guessed to be sixteen. She wore a clean dress with her thick black hair pulled back into a ponytail. She had grown up in the orphanage and was quiet and shy. The other worker was twenty but seemed mentally slow, lacking in some of her senses. Her clothes were that of a laborer -navy blue pants and a gray buttoned-down shirt. Her dark brown hair was cropped to her earlobes and had probably never felt the bristles of a brush. Her eyes darted back and forth and her crooked smile left me wondering if she was smiling with me or at me.

As we set off, Cindy took the lead, and I pulled up the rear with Yu Yan in my arms. I had brought cheese nips and cookies from Hong Kong so that I could offer the children a few snacks at the park.

We arrived five minutes later at a small grassy area surrounded by tall trees. A muddy round indentation in the ground looked like the remnants of a pond. A small circular concrete table surrounded by four stools was situated under the trees, and we unpacked our simple foods and toys. Cindy had purchased toy airplanes and balls that the older children played with.

I observed the joy and laughter that the children expressed as they ran and played with their simple entertainment. No passerby would have any idea that in an hour these children would be tucked away on the fourth floor of a dark concrete building. For now, though, they looked like local children.

Yu Yan sat on one of the stools and showed no signs of wanting to interact. I crouched in front of her and tried to engage her in simple activities. I raised my hands and sang, "Clap hands, clap hands till mummy comes home." She did not attempt to mimic my action. Her eyes remained blank and uninterested.

I thought. *What will it take to gain a response from her?*

CHAPTER 9

AN ANGEL

December arrived with festivities in abundance and the spirit of Christmas in the air. My parents flew in from Canada and would remain until our final departure in February.

I booked my last journey into Zhaoqing before the auction. My mother decided to go with me. Her decision reflected her unfailing support, which had been prevalent throughout my life. She watched a video of the orphanage and got excited at the prospect of meeting her new granddaughter.

My father opted out of the visit. He pulled me aside. "Lee, I'm not comfortable in such harsh environments, but I want you to know that I'm fully behind what you're doing."

I smiled. "Dad, that's fine, you'll meet Yu Yan soon enough."

As we arrived in port, the wind whistled, sending a chill through the air. A sense of comfort swept through me as mum and I made our way towards the hotel. Even though I was a minority in a foreign city, with my mother by my side and the excitement of my new daughter beckoning, I had much to be grateful for. I was in the midst of experiencing an exhilarating phenomenon on multiple levels. The adrenaline rush was uncontrollable. The adoption was underway. The auction was a week away and the donations coming in were amazing. The opportunity to renovate the orphanage would be the cherry on top, the gold at the end of the rainbow.

After we unpacked I tried to locate my translator Erin, but discovered that she was away for the week. I hadn't thought to contact her before our arrival. My heart sank; how irresponsible. There were topics related to the proceeds from the auction and our adoptions that I wanted to discuss with the orphanage director before my January visit.

I stood leaning on the hotel's front desk inquiring about a western restaurant when I overheard a young Chinese man speaking with an Australian accent. He was dressed in tailored khaki pants with a starched black, long-sleeved, button-down shirt and wearing black leather loafers, not the faded blue or brown cotton pants rolled above the ankle with a solid shirt and simple cloth shoes. The customary attire of men in Zhaoqing His face was fresh and animated.

"I hear a slight accent." I said to him. "You're not from Zhaoqing."

With a big smile and clear accent, he turned to me. "Well, neither are you. At least I blend in with the crowds."

I laughed. "Touché. Was it my height or color of hair that gave it away?"

He gave me a once-over look. "Actually, your eyes."

I continued. "What brings you to this bustling town?"

"I've been living in Australia for the past ten years and recently returned to China to start a business. You're far from home. Foreign women are not a common sight in this city. What's your story?"

"I visit once a month to help out at the orphanage. I'm also in the process of trying to adopt a little girl." I wanted to ask him to help me with translations, but I held back, uncomfortable asking a stranger.

It was like he was reading my thoughts and on cue he said, "Do you need help? I'm fluent in Mandarin and have no schedule for the day."

I wanted to hug him. "That would be fantastic. Are you sure I'm not imposing on you?"

"No worries. I'd love to help. You'll show me a part of the city I didn't know existed. I'm Ken, and you are?"

"Lee." I reached out to shake his hand. "Nice to meet you."

My mother, Ken and I arrived at the orphanage and it was like walking into an old black and white movie; the grey tones of the film replaying the same scene time and time again. The director greeted us with a pleasant smile and gestured us toward the fourth floor. Ken spoke with her explaining my intention to adopt Yu Yan. He told her an auction to raise funds for the orphanage was planned and the money raised would refurbish the fourth floor. She nodded, looked at me and kept smiling.

The children were dressed in their entire wardrobe hoping to warm their frail bodies. Yu Yan was slumped over the walker, lost in her own world. She was layered in pants with a pair of bright red sweatpants on the outside. She wore two shirts and a jade green sweatshirt with an embroidered elephant in festive colors. Her little feet were bare and icy to the touch. I requested some socks and one of the workers scurried into the back room and produced a well-worn pair. At this point anything would help. I found her a pair of shoes and placing them on her feet was as hard as putting flip-flops on a duck. I took her out of the walker.

When Yu Yan stood, she clung to the side of the bed and did not move. I took her hand and coaxed her slowly towards the door. Her tiny cold fingers held mine as she fell into her shuffle walk. She took small steps, the soles of her feet shifting along the tile floor. We made our way into the main room, where she was content to remain standing.

Ken walked up to me. "Do a lot of these children get adopted?"

I shrugged. "It's hard to tell. I've been coming here for the last five months and all the older kids are still here. It's difficult to keep track of the babies. I haven't seen many babies move into the big room. I think a lot of the little ones don't make it."

His eyes widened. "Don't make it?"

"I think they get sick from lack of care. Going to the hospital is not an option. If the workers can't cure the child, he or she will eventually die. Don't quote me on this, but I've seen a lot of the babies disappear from the nursery month to month. I asked once where they went. The director told me they were adopted, but I'm not so sure."

He walked toward the director and began a conversation.

The door to the dying room was open. I casually walked by and peeked in. To my relief, there were no children in there.

Meanwhile, my mum gathered her bearings. She picked up Yu Yan, who spontaneously wrapped her legs around my mother's waist. Yu Yan remained placid in her lap as they both sat and watched the other children. I took out coloring books and crayons and passed them round to create a little diversion in their monotonous day. The children immersed themselves in the activity.

An hour later the ever-dependable doctor arrived and presented her booklet charting Yu Yan's progress. It was filled with Chinese characters. Her dedication and diligence with Yu Yan was evident

I introduced Ken who nodded to the woman and spoke in Mandarin. He turned to me. "The doctor visits twice a day." His tone showed his surprise. "Her notes explain the activities she does with Yu Yan."

The three of us departed with the doctor and walked toward the hotel. Along the way I slipped the doctor an envelope with four hundred Hong Kong dollars. Ken was patient and never indicated a need to leave. The doctor turned to him and they exchanged a few words.

He looked over at me. "The doctor would like you to bring her a camera instead of money next month."

I did not hesitate in my response. "Of course. Please tell her how thankful I am for all that she has done. I'll be back on January 22."

At the hotel I offered to pay Ken. He shook his head and said, "This was a great day for me. Thank you. You are doing wonderful things."

I shook his hand. "You really saved my day. I didn't know how I was going to communicate with the director. Thanks for all your help."

I was astounded how a stranger had entered my life and come to my aid willingly. Fate had brought us together at that particular minute at the front desk. He unselfishly opened his heart to me, contributing his time and help. I felt like an angel from above had flown down from the heavens and touched my life. Our paths crossed briefly and then he departed from my life as quickly as he had entered it.

My mum and I dined at a nearby hotel that featured western cuisine. In retrospect, it would be the same as someone from China arriving in Los Angeles craving Chinese food, to be taken to Mr. Wong's for egg foo yung and chow mein, neither of which is found on a normal menu in mainland China. I decided to be safe and order fried chicken with rice. Unbeknownst to me, an entire chicken arrived, head still intact and fried. My mum opted for noodles with vegetables that arrived without any surprises, much to her relief.

The next day we had a quick breakfast and headed to the orphanage for a visit before boarding the noon ferry. The children greeted us with smiling faces, and I handed out the remainder of the pictures to color. I spent a little time helping Yu Yan with her walking.

At eleven o'clock there was a scampering of feet as we watched mealtime unfold. The children brought out the two weather-beaten green tables and the children fetched a chair and placed it around the table. One of the older girls arrived with two stainless steel bowls balancing on top of each other. Another young girl followed close behind with blue plastic bowls stacked high. She handed them out to each child along with a spoon. The two girls proceeded to serve one spoonful of rice into each bowl and then a spoonful of steamed, leafy vegetables with a few fragments of meat tossed in. The children all consumed the food in a flash. Not a grain of rice was left. Even the eighteen-year-old boy who suffered from cerebral palsy and did not have the use of his hands immersed his face into the bowl and devoured his meal.

It crossed my mind that snacks would be a novelty to these children. They were given three meals a day and had learned early on to eat whatever was placed before them. I thought of children growing up in North American and wondered how many children at two years old looked forward to a small bowl of rice and vegetables for lunch. Within moments of finishing their food, like a trained militia, these children stacked the bowls, shoved their chairs into the corner, and pushed the tables over to the side. At no point did a worker issue a command or gesture.

Yu Yan was now a lot like the other children. Walking around, doing her part of the daily chores. I had hoped to see a flicker of acknowledgement when she saw me, but that was not to be.

CHAPTER 10

CHINA'S CHILDREN

The remainder of December moved rapidly as the auction took form and plans were being finalized. Miguel and I had accumulated a diverse array of auction items. The auction items ranged from pottery, to a fly from Kai Tak Airport to a landing on an aircraft carrier, to weekends in Guam.

We started to gather all the items and experience what began as an idea three months earlier, blossom in front of us.

Two weeks prior to the auction, Miguel and I gathered with good friends for a farewell meal at Casa Mexicana Restaurant. The place served food that elevated Taco Bell onto a pedestal, but the atmosphere was electric and the margaritas potent.

The lead singer of the band playing announced that a special guest was dining in the restaurant and had promised to sing a few songs. Maria Cordero took the microphone. She was one of Hong Kong's leading vocalists. She sang with a vibrant, distinctive voice and everyone there was mesmerized. I looked over at Miguel and, as if via osmosis, I could tell the same thought had crossed through his mind.

Miguel walked around the table to me. "We can at least ask. If she says no we are no worse off."

I nodded.

I thought in life, that you should ask. I had been positively surprised enough times that I felt the attempt to be worth it.

I watched Miguel when he approached Maria after she completed her performance. He explained our auction to her and what we hoped to accomplish.

"Would you be willing to help us? It'd be great to have you sing before dinner."

"Tell me the place and time. I love a good cause." She answered.

Miguel came back beaming. "It's going to be an incredible auction and evening."

Though the auction was moving along well, the adoption wasn't. Miguel and I were once again having problems with the authentication of our documents. He faxed the following letter to Ms. Liu and followed up with a telephone call a few days later.

Dear Ms. Liu,

First and foremost I would like to thank you for listening to our case and being so helpful to us. I am sorry to have to trouble you again, however, we are encountering some difficulties in reference to an adoption case that you have been advising us on.

As you may recall I have been in contact with you on numerous occasions regarding our adopting a handicapped little girl from an orphanage in Zhaoqing, China. I faxed you a letter concerning this situation and a diagnosis given to us by a doctor of the condition of Goo Yu Yan. In addition to this I contacted you recently because the Chinese Consulate in Los Angeles would not authenticate our home study because they said that my wife and I were not over 35 years of age.

The letter continued to state that a personal phone call from Ms. Liu to the Chinese Consulate in Los Angeles was necessary in order for our adoption process to proceed.

On January 7, two weeks later we received a letter from Wide Horizons for Children, which was the umbrella organization that Kay (who did our home study) worked for and was also a US adoption agency.

The letter explained that the Ministry of Justice and Civil Affairs offices were joining together to create a new body, The China International Adoption Organization. The organization was still in the process of being formed. All completed document packets would be submitted to the CIAO once it was functioning.

Therefore, there would be a backlog as the CIAO would be facing a monumental task once they began reviewing the many dossiers that had been submitted.

These new changes created mixed emotions; I didn't know what this meant to our application, as we were not represented by an adoption agency. It would be the waiting game again as we had no control of expediting the process.

Patience became the only option.

The next two weeks were a blend of meetings and attending to last-minute auction details. My parents had been a constant source of love and strength in my life and I felt truly blessed to have them. My parents filled in all the slots with the girls while I tied up the final touches with the auction.

The day of the auction arrived and I was soaring like a comet in the night sky. I left the apartment at 8:30 a.m., telling my parents that I'd be home in time to shower and return with them to the auction.

With my to-do list in hand, I walked up the club steps. I had arranged to filter the funds we raised through Youth With a Mission because it was a registered charity. I would still have control of disbursing the funds. I compiled a list of items that I wanted for the Zhaoqing orphanage. We would be purchasing cribs for the nursery, beds for the dormitory, a washer, a rice cooker, blankets, paint and warm winter jackets for all the children.

Cindy, Jennifer and my dear friend Teresa greeted me at the reception desk. They had volunteered their time to wrap up the final details.

Cindy handed me a sheet of paper. "Here's your opening speech. I suggest you read through it a few times so you will be comfortable with my writing."

I scanned the words and looked up at her. "Thanks. I get nervous speaking in front of people."

Cindy patted me on the shoulder. "Better you than me."

I laughed. "Oh, thanks, that's helpful."

Teresa held out a stack of programs. "What's the next step with these?"

"A yellow ribbon needs to be tied through the holes and a bid number written on the back." I replied.

"OK, I've got that covered." Teresa turned and headed up the stairs.

I looked over at Jennifer. "Would you mind handling the silent auction tables? The items need to be displayed on the tables outside the foyer and the bid sheets need to be attached in front."

She smiled back. "OK, I can handle that."

I took Cindy's advice and headed up to the main dining room to practice my speech. My stomach knotted when I stood before a group. I was conscious of my accent and how fast my words tumbled out. I stood behind the podium and read aloud my lines a few times.

I looked at the clock. The day had vanished. An hour remained before the auction.

I called my mother. "There's no way I can make it back to the apartment. Would you mind bringing my clothes when you and Dad come?"

Her ever-calming voice was reassuring. "That's fine. The girls are fed and Remy is reading them a story. We are leaving now."

Remy was our live-in housekeeper, which was one of the affordable luxuries of living in Asia. "Please give the girls a hug and kiss for me. I'll meet you in the lobby."

I had envisioned styling my hair to portray a semblance of togetherness, but that was a fleeting thought earlier in the day. My parents arrived and I rushed upstairs to dress.

I took a deep breath and walked upstairs to the main dining room to welcome the one hundred and twenty guests. I ascended the staircase with trepidation, my emotions in a whirlwind. I was dumbfounded that this day had actually arrived. Three months prior it was a simple wish-a thought, a dream. Now, it was time to live it. I was thrilled. I would be able to spread a little warmth into the hearts of a few underprivileged children. I entered the doors to the main dining room and a spark ignited within me.

The panoramic view from the main dining room was breathtaking. Twenty- foot, floor-to-ceiling windows invited guests to absorb exotic shorelines and the Pacific Ocean that stretched to the horizon. And then there was the lush green mountains rolled toward the water's edge, ending with the rocky terrain that protected the island from the waves that crashed the shores. The room looked lovely. White tablecloths covered each table, with a centerpiece of fresh yellow roses. The banner "China's Children" hung above the podium and a small wooden dance floor had been laid in front of the three-man band.

Looking dapper in his tuxedo, Marty Gooseen paced the floor. He caught my eye and walked over. "I hope you're ready for this, my dear." He smiled, his eyes dancing with energy.

"I better be!" I replied, trying to calm the churning in my stomach.

Miguel walked in, dressed handsomely in one of his tailored suits. In his managerial tone, he took charge of the conversation. "I want to make sure we're all on the same page."

"Run the itinerary by me one more time to make sure I'm on track," Marty replied as we all huddled together.

"The cocktails will be served in the foyer at seven-thirty as guests are submitting their bids for the silent auction. A dinner bell will ring at eight so everyone can be seated in the main dining area. At that point, Lee will go to the podium. The screen to her left will show photographs of the orphanage. Marty will then introduce Maria, who agreed to sing Whitney Houston's, "The Greatest Love of All." Hopefully by then, the entrée will be served and dessert will be on the way. At that point, Marty, you are the man of the hour and will take control of the mike and make people throw their money at you."

Marty smiled and put his hand on Miguel's shoulder. "Sounds like you have things under control. I'm ready to roll. I think lots of wallets will open up wide tonight."

I stood before both men and put my arms around them. "Well, guys, it's time to make this happen. Marty, thanks again for allowing us to coerce you into this. I'm excited."

He squeezed my arm. "My absolute pleasure. It's going to be fun."

I retreated to the foyer. It was time to play the enchanting hostess and make sure all the pieces fell into place. I took another deep breath and began a memorable evening.

The curtains were drawn and the performers took the stage. On cue, the guests arrived; they mingled in the foyer and browsed along the silent auction tables investigating the wares. Guests were dressed in true Hong Kong fashion; a parade of designer labels. The Chanel suits and Cole Hahn pumps strolled by with Gucci and Fendi bags clutched in manicured hands. The Mikimoto pearls perfectly wrapped porcelain necks, and diamond tennis bracelets shimmered on wrists. The men dressed in their tailored suits with monograms on their French cuff sleeves and gold cuff links peeking through.

Bids were placed and chatter filled the room. Everyone filtered into the dining room and located their seats. I wandered around the room, making polite conversation and giving assistance.

Marty found the spotlight and the play unfolded. I was signaled to approach the podium. I clutched my notes in hand, took a deep breath, parted my lips and prayed that my vocal chords cooperated. I fiddled with the microphone and began my speech. The words slowly fell out.

"Dear Friends, Your attendance at this evening's China's Children Benefit is important. Through your participation and the generosity of several corporations and individuals, the proceeds from this evening's auction will be used to purchase food, medical supplies, clothing and beds for children for whom these gifts may mean the difference between life and death.

Each day in mainland China, countless numbers of babies are abandoned and left to die. Without the resources or manpower to handle so many desperate children, the orphanages are unable to save all these babies and many are allowed to die from preventable causes such as hunger, exposure and simple childhood illnesses. There are no exact figures on how many children are abandoned in China. A study published by Swedish demographers in 1991, however, discovered there were at least 700,000 "missing" baby girls among China's more than 20 million annual births.

This evening's proceeds will go to Youth With a Mission, a registered Hong Kong charity that is doing remarkable work on behalf of the orphans in China.

The number of children and babies in China's orphanages is overwhelming, the needs are staggering. We believe that a difference can be made, by helping save one life at a time. With your help, we can help several children by improving the quality of care they receive. All children deserve the chance for a life filled with hope and dignity.

Thank you for helping us gives this gift. Have a wonderful evening."

I chopped a few sentences in half, but was able to talk with clarity and make occasional eye contact. I concluded my monologue; my lips curled upward, smiling, more out of relief than protocol.

Maria took center stage, obviously comfortable with an audience. She improvised Whitney Houston's song, to incorporate children of China in the verses. Her vocal chords were well rehearsed and her strong, vibrant voice penetrated the room. The slides flashed behind her depicting the life in the Zhaoqing orphanage.

Once the applause subsided, Marty regained the spotlight and assumed the auctioneer's role. "The first item up for auction is a Porsche black leather bag. Let's start the bidding at one thousand Hong Kong dollars (US$130)."

The room filled with electricity. I circled the room as a spotter, my feet barely making contact with the carpet. Marty was cajoling and entertaining the crowd, the description of each items rolled off his tongue, he did not miss a beat. We were surrounded by wealth; disposable income was everywhere and the members contributed a fair share to the cause.

Finally, item number twenty, two-round trip tickets and a four-night stay at the Pacific Island Club in Guam. By night's end, Marty's voice was hoarse, my feet were blistered and we raised more than $45,000 US, I was ecstatic. The adrenaline continued to pump through my veins.

It was now 12:15 a.m. and we would be heading to Zhaoqing in nine hours to refurbish the orphanage. I looked around. The chairs were now empty, the napkins stained, remnants of coffee had settled in the china cups and the red lipstick marks were imprinted on the crystal glasses. I landed back on earth, still embracing the experience of a truly wondrous night.

People from different arenas had pitched in their talents, time and energy. It had been a big jigsaw puzzle that needed lots of pieces to fall together to create the final masterpiece.

Silently, I thanked them all - the American Club staff who contributed the banner, the florist who donated the centerpieces, Richard Ross who allowed it to happen, Philipe Sieler who provided a delectable meal, Cindy who gave her time and writing skills, Jenny who marketed the tickets, my parents who watched the girls during the chaotic week, Maria Cordero who unselfishly provided the entertainment with the Club Band, Marty who brought it all together and the guests who donated generously. Last, I closed my eyes and thanked Miguel who threw himself wholeheartedly into his wife's crazy idea.

CHAPTER 11

PLAYING FAIRY GODMOTHER

The morning after the auction came too quickly. After our late night, Miguel and I rose at six to meet our friend Jim Sorlie, who had volunteered his weekend to come and help paint the orphanage. Jim was six-foot-two, with sparse strands of wheat-colored hair combed over his crown. His jovial demeanor brought a smile to my face and warmth to my heart. His round spectacles rested on the bridge of his nose giving him the look of an intellectual teddy bear.

Exhilaration filtered through me, like a child at the carnival. This would be my last journey into Zhaoqing before our final departure from Hong Kong to Florida.

I had never consumed drugs, but no form of artificial stimulant could duplicate the natural high that I was experiencing. I had reached a pinnacle of achievement by raising enough money to make a difference in several orphanages. Tomorrow, I'd embark upon a forty-eight hour spending frenzy in which I had the power to bring comfort and color into these orphans' dreary lives.

We arrived in the bustling, familiar town and went directly to the orphanage. The director accompanied me to the local department store while Jim and Miguel went in search of paints and supplies. I was enjoying the ability to play the role of fairy godmother for a day and grant these children wishes. We ordered blue metal cribs for the nursery, purple metal beds for the dormitory, blankets, a washer, rice cooker and warm jackets for all the children. I attempted to cover all possible needs and selfishly enjoyed the uplifting rush that carved permanent smile on my face. We arrived back at the orphanage to observe Miguel and Jim busily painting the interior walls. The place began to shine. Everyone pitched in and we worked late into the afternoon.

Yu Yan was becoming more independent. She had relinquished her statue-like poses and begun to mingle with her peers. Her steps were still slow and controlled, but she had acquired freedom. But, her poker face remained intact, and she made no sounds. She had mastered her own sign language, gesturing for her needs.

In my interview Kay the social worker had planted a small seed of doubt, but I was learning to trust my gut instinct. Yu Yan had an innate strength to survive, but no medical books would reinforce my diagnosis. So, I went with blind, unconditional faith in a child with no history and a dubious medical record.

The doctor passed by on her way home and asked what hotel room we were staying in as she planned to stop by with her husband later that evening. We were leaving when the director approached me with Yu Yan in her arms, gesturing that I could take her for the night. I was touched and opened my arms to receive Yu Yan.

Worn out, sleep deprived and hungry, we headed back to the hotel, our eyes twinkling with satisfaction.

Yu Yan's legs instantly coiled around my waist and she quickly wrapped her arms around my shoulders. It was like holding an overstuffed doll. Yu Yan weighed seventeen pounds and we figured she was two years old. She did not utter a sound on the walk to the hotel but her eyes darted around observing the scenery.

A stale smell of urine followed us into the hotel room. I took pleasure in filling the bath, pouring in shower gel and immersing Yu Yan's tiny body into the warm water. Her vocal chords opened and without words she expressed her dislike for the water. She scrunched up her face and yelled.

Her tiny torso told a tale of its own. Her stomach was distended and covered with a fine red rash. The scars from the infected cuts remained on her hips as a constant reminder of her discomforts from those elastic bands around her waist. I could circle my thumb and index finger around her little leg that protruded awkwardly from beneath her belly. Her jet black hair lay limp on her forehead, her bangs cut straight across - the true definition of a bowl cut. Miguel came into the bathroom, and wrapped her shivering body in a towel. She seemed to relax and find comfort in the warmth of his body as he held her.

"She's so small." Miguel remarked

"I bet you she'll gain weight quickly. I can't imagine leaving her behind not knowing when we'll see her again." I said.

Miguel tucked Yu Yan under the covers. Her dark eyes showed no emotion. This was her first time sleeping on a mattress. She didn't squirm or look uncomfortable.

I gently kissed her forehead. "Sleep tight my little princess."

At 7:15 p.m. there was a soft tapping on the door. The doctor and her husband stood outside. I went to the adjacent room where Jim was staying and asked him to be present during the conversation. I led our guest's into Jim's room.

I had bought the small automatic Nikon camera that she had requested. I sat on the edge of the bed beside Jim. The doctor and her husband sat facing us in two wooden chairs. I handed her the camera and her smile showed gratitude. I told her that Jim spoke Mandarin and they could attempt to communicate through him. She looked at Jim and rattled off sentences in Mandarin.

A look of discomfort crossed his face as he turned to me, "I'm not sure I want to translate what she's saying."

Curiosity took precedence, "Jim, whatever she said is fine. I'm sure I can handle it."

Miguel had entered the room and sat beside me on the bed.

"Lee, the doctor is implying that you should not adopt Yu Yan. She has too many medical problems."

Miguel shifted closer and put his arms around my shoulders.

Puzzled, I looked at the doctor, "Jim, it's irrelevant to us what she thinks. We're confident in whatever ailments Yu Yan has, we can manage them." Jim relayed the message.

"Don't be upset. Let the doctor talk." Miguel said his voice calm when he spoke.

The doctor in turn, answered through Jim, "She says that you deserve better. There are a lot of healthy babies at the orphanage that would bring you more happiness."

At this point my mind conjured up visions of the doctor inhibiting Yu Yan's adoption. I forced a smile and said to Jim, "Try to explain to her that Yu Yan is the one we love deeply and are looking forward to helping her."

A smile crossed the doctor's face and she began again. Jim smiled, "She says you have a big heart and that Yu Yan is a lucky girl."

Miguel squeezed me and then winked.

I returned the smile and bowed my head as a gesture of appreciation for her comment, "Jim, please emphasize my thanks to her for her help."

The doctor's small heart-shaped mouth curled up, she stood, her husband following, and they left the room.

I looked over at Jim, "Now that was bizarre. And a little gutsy on her part to voice her opinion."

Jim inhaled a small breath; "I think she felt obliged to state her feelings. She's a good honest woman."

"You know, I may be acting naïve, but my intuition is telling me that Yu Yan is going to be healthy. I see her strength when I look into her eyes. I guess time will answer the questions."

Jim smiled and patted me on the shoulder as I walked out.

I tiptoed over to the tiny torso tucked into the bed beside ours. Her little eyes were shut tight. I wondered what thoughts had crossed her innocent mind before she fell asleep. She was alone in a new environment with two strangers. Did she know how different her life would be?

"See, no need to worry. Everything will work out in the end." Miguel spoke as he slid under the covers. He reached over and kissed me goodnight.

Sleep came easily. When my head met the pillow my body deflated and blended into the mattress beneath me. A blackness enveloped me, and I drifted off into a deep slumber.

The next day Jim, Miguel, Yu Yan and I returned to the orphanage to finish the painting and to receive delivery of the goods we purchased from the day before. A buzz filled the air as we all got to work, cleaning and getting ready for the delivery. All of the old furniture had already been removed when we arrived. The nursery and bedroom were swept and mopped, and the walls freshly painted.

When the truck arrived everyone including the children helped unload and set up the new furniture. They beamed as they inspected their new jackets and furniture. Blue cribs and purple beds were installed and the orphanage looked happier. By eleven o'clock, the new items were in place. We all stood back to admire the facelift. I felt guilty for the immense sense of contentment and happiness that flowed through my body. As St. Francis of Assisi said, "For it is in the giving, that we receive."

I picked up Yu Yan and held her in my lap. She molded to my body and sat quietly, looking at the activities around her. For a child of two, she was complex. After all this time, I had yet to see her smile. I tried tickling her toes and under her arms, but to no avail.

No attempt at words ever escaped her lips. She expressed either a solemn look or a scream of discontent, that was her emotional range. I even tried to sneak up behind her and scare her, but Yu Yan did not flinch. I knew that I had to accept the possibility that she may have developmental disabilities, but in my heart I chose not to believe it.

I had hoped that Yu Yan would be joining us in February, but the political jockeying in Beijing continued. Even though the culmination of hours that I had spent with Yu Yan over the past year was minimal, I felt responsibility for her. I wanted to relay to her that her life would be OK, that I would return and take her away, that she would smile and laugh with her new sisters and would grow to understand the meaning of love. I wanted to give her hope, security and love that would last forever

I embraced Yu Yan tightly then placed her down in front of me as I knelt. I looked directly into her charcoal eyes.

"I love you. I promise I'll l be back to take you home." The tears collect in the corner of my eyes. Her eyes showed no acknowledgement of my words. I said good-bye with a heavy heart and made my departure. I had no idea when I would return, but I knew that I would.

We headed back to the hotel to collect our bags and head to the ferry terminal. Once on board I sighed deeply, feeling weary but fully satisfied with our completed mission. We didn't change the world, but we had made a difference in the lives of a few people.

The next few weeks were a whirlwind. The packers arrived on February 12, and we moved into the Victoria Hotel. In a week our family would be back in Florida. A chapter of my life had closed. I had resided in Hong Kong for four and a half years. I arrived young and energetic and ready to conquer the world. I was leaving with a resume filled with experiences and adventure. We had immersed ourselves in the Asian culture, learning to eat with chopsticks and learning to understand the nuances of their traditions.

While in China, Miguel and I had explored the peasant villages on bicycles with two dear friends. We had witnessed dogs being skinned for food.

We had traveled to Beijing, where we walked through the halls of history at the Forbidden City. We had climbed the stone stairs of the Great Wall of China and stood in Tiananmen Square, where protestors' blood had been shed for human rights.   We had also visited the islands of the Philippines where we were enchanted by the charisma and warmth of its people.

It had been an unforgettable time, memories that will remain ingrained for a lifetime, experiences that changed our lives. We had arrived as Asian novices and were leaving as veterans.

And we hoped our family would be one precious child larger.

CHAPTER 12

1994 JACKSONVILLE, FLORIDA

After a sixteen-hour flight Miguel and I touched down in Jacksonville, Florida holding the hands of two tired little girls. We entered the terminal and I heard a friendly Delta representative's voice saying, "Welcome to Jacksonville, enjoy your stay." The social interaction caught me off guard; in Hong Kong no one exchanges friendly banter. I looked up with a big smile on my face and replied, "Thank you so much I hope you have a nice day." I was home.

Our house had been rented out and we would be living in an apartment for six months until the family moved out.

Miguel would be embarking on his dream of being an entrepreneur and was in the process of opening his own coffee shop, Java Café. He had spent months researching coffee and had visited Seattle, where the coffee industry was booming.

We remained in touch with Mrs. Liu from the government offices in Beijing but our last contact had been unnerving because she didn't take our call. Apparently the two government factions were still fighting for control of the adoptions. Until that was resolved, all cases remained on hold.

In March, we re-established communication with her, at which point she requested that we translate our documents into Mandarin, making two copies and mailing her the originals. We called in a favor from a good friend in Hong Kong, Sue Baker, who was a lawyer. She arranged for the translations to be done. During the whole adoption process we were constantly reminded of the true value of friendships. So many people had pitched in to help us. We would be eternally grateful to them.

On June 26, 1994, eight months after we began the adoption process, we got final verbal approval from China that all our documents were in order and would be mailed to Guangzhou. Our adoption had been approved and it was time to bring Yu Yan home. An appointment was scheduled at The Ministry of Justice in Guangzhou in July for us to collect the written approval.

Guangzhou is a metropolis on the Pearl River in southern China. Once known as Canton, it is now the most important industrial and foreign trade center in the south. It has become the most prosperous city under China's "open-to-the-outside-world" policy. With a population of sixty million people, it is a tropical land of fish farms, brimming rice paddy fields and bustling villages. It is a two-hour train ride from Zhaoqing.

I would be traveling back to China alone. Miguel was in the midst of renovating the coffee shop and finalizing all the logistics. The trip into China would not be a smooth journey. All the patience I possessed had to be tapped in order to endure the two-week process. My mother was flying down from Canada to stay with the girls while I was away. This would be the first time I had ever left the girls for such a long period. My heart felt heavy.

My ebony and ivory daughters. Sierra was two and a half and Havana was eighteen months old. Sierra was an identical stamp of me. Her charcoal eyes were outlined with long lashes and thick, dark eyebrows, which accentuated her olive complexion. Her long dark brown strands touched her shoulders. She was independent and strong-willed. She pranced around in her underwear and took delight in creating wardrobes from scarves and bandanas.

Havana awoke each morning with a twinkle in her eye. Her blonde, Shirley Temple curls sprang to their own music, framing her Bambi brown eyes and small ski- jump nose.

Havana was carefree and loved the outdoors. I remembered once when my parents were visiting and my father was weeding outside, Havana came into the kitchen to get a spoon to help weed. That night we were sitting down to dinner. I served corn on the cob. Havana sat focused on her corn, and then pulling out a string from between the corn rows, she held it up and said, "Mum, look, the corn has weeds!"

I had a photograph of Yu Yan on the fridge and spoke of her to the girls. Miguel and I had decided to give her a western name but wanted a connection with her hometown, Zhaoqing. We decided to name her Zhoe.

A week before I left, I sat with them on the couch. Havana climbed onto my lap and I pulled Sierra in close with my left arm around her shoulder. I had the photograph of Zhoe in my right hand.

"Girls, remember how I told you that one day I'd have to go to China to pick up your sister and bring her home."

In unison they replied and nodded, "Yes, mum."

Sierra looked up at me, "Is she ready to come home?"

Havana was squirming on my lap and twirling my hair. "Yes, she is."

Havana began bouncing up and down. Sierra started to clap her hands and jumped off the couch yelling, "Zhoe's coming hommme."

I calmed them down and pulled both close. "Girls, Zhoe will be shy. And, she doesn't speak."

Sierra chirped in, "I can teach her."

"Me too." Smiled Havana.

My heart fluttered. I hope you can, I thought, and I hope Zhoe will respond. "You two will be good teachers. Grandma is coming to visit while I go to China."

Sierra got serious. "How long will you be gone? Can I come too?"

I hugged them tightly. "No my love, mum has to go alone. I'll be gone for fourteen sleeps."

CHAPTER 13

1994 – JULY - FINAL JOURNEY

Five months after leaving Asia I arrived back into Hong Kong. The all-too-familiar landing - descending from the clouds as the nose of the plane dove towards the Pacific waters, followed by the screeching sounds of landing gear contacting with the runway. The sixteen-hour journey from Florida was over.

I flew into Hong Kong first because I had to apply for a Chinese visa and then I'd take a ferry into Guangzhou to complete the adoption process.

I located the long taxi line and the humidity wrapped around me like a furry blanket. My friends Chip and Sue Baker invited me to stay with them for the two nights I'd be in the city. Anxiety crept in as the overcrowded streets and noise pollution once again surrounded me. The energy I once fed off of now felt like a fifty-pound weight on my shoulders.

Chip and Sue lived in the Mid-Levels, half-way between the South Coast and Central, as downtown Hong Kong was known. I walked up the stairs, tugging my duffel bag behind me as I climbed to the third floor. Sue's smiling face greeted me with a cold bottle of beer in her hand. We embraced, "It's great to see you."

Chip, the constant jester, was close behind with his warm smile. "Well, well, well, I guess you were going through pollution withdrawals. Did you need to inhale some of this Asian fragrance once more?"

"Actually, it was the warmth of the people I missed." I grinned, then added, "and the spacious living."

Their apartment was like the majority of young expatriates apartments. It was seven hundred and fifty square feet, a kitchenette tucked into the corner on the right, a small bathroom that one slid into sideways to enter, a bedroom in the back and a combination living- dining room in the front. The décor of rosewood furniture and carved Buddha's reflected their travels in Asia and created a comfortable and homey atmosphere.

The jet lag was taking its toll and I flopped down on the couch. "Here I am, back in Hong Kong. There were times I thought I'd have to smuggle Yu Yan across the border."

"I'm sorry we won't be here on your return. I'd like to put a face to all the stories we've heard." Chip said.

Sue handed me some Chinese phrases written on a piece of paper. "I asked my secretary to write down common phrases for you and the addresses in Guangzhou that you will need. I hope you brought a lot of patience with you. Not speaking Mandarin will be frustrating. You know the Chinese have no concept of time. Be prepared to play the waiting game."

"Thanks. Yes, Mick warned me. Not to mention the fact that I'm a female alone. He said to speak firmly in my requests and to be pushy. Being a foreigner should work in my favor."

I retraced my old steps downtown and applied for my visa and booked my ferry into China.

With Chinese phrases in hand and duffel bag drooped over my shoulder, I arrived in Guangzhou on July 7 at 11:30 a.m. A wave of insecurity overtook me as I realized I was in a foreign city carrying $5000 in traveler's checks. The blistering sun was directly overhead and the hustling of workers engulfed me. I raised my arm and waved for a taxi. When a driver stopped I handed him the address to my first stop, the Ministry of Justice to collect my approved adoption papers. He looked in the rearview mirror and gave me a crooked smile, exposing his yellow teeth.

I entered a drab concrete building that was sparsely furnished with two benches in the lobby. I climbed the steps to the second floor.

The Chinese official was balding with black glasses sitting on his nose. He was neatly dressed in a gray suit. He raised his eyes and met mine as I introduced myself. He spoke broken English. He handed me documentation and then said, "You need go Civil Affairs Office. It not open until three."

He handed me the address and continued. "Official from Zhaoqing in Guangzhou, he take you Zhaoqing after."

His helpfulness impressed me but I remained uneasy with the thought of driving through the back roads of China with a man I didn't know and couldn't communicate with. I envisioned being whisked away into one of the remote villages in the north.

It was now 12:30 p.m. To make use of time I decided to go to the US Consulate and find information on the immigration process. Once I completed the Chinese paperwork I'd have to return there to apply for Yu Yan's United States visa. When I arrived, I saw the consulate was closed until 2:00 p.m. I passed a long-distance telephone booth and decided to call Miguel. A combination of jet lag, anxiety and the frustration made my vocal chords freeze when I heard his voice. "Miguel ..."

"Lee, where are you? Are you crying? Are you OK? Talk to me."

I became an emotional mess, and struggled to compose myself. I knew he'd start to panic, as the distance magnified the smallest problem. After thirty seconds of releasing every teardrop I possessed, I inhaled deeply.

"I'm sorry. I didn't mean to worry you. My mind is churning with all the details. I got a message that a government worker is coming to take me to Zhaoqing."

"Lee, under no circumstances should you go in the car. There'll be no way of tracking you."

"I know. I'll have to see what happens."

"Make sure and call me when you arrive at the hotel in Zhaoqing."

"I will. I'll talk to you later."

I replaced the receiver and thought: rule number one: don't call when you're emotional.

I arrived at the Civil Affairs Department at 3:00 p.m. It's building was a duplicate of the Ministry of Justice building. The stark interior displayed four desks lined up parallel to the window, a couch, two chairs and a coffee table on the other side of the room. There was one man in the office. He spoke English. He asked a few questions and started filling out forms.

"Mrs. Zhang Xia Qiang is arriving at five." The Chinese official stated.

"Oh, I didn't know she was going to meet me here." The knot in my stomach loosened.

Mrs. Qiang, the orphanage director, arrived at five thirty with Yu Yan and three other people from the Civil Affairs Office in Zhaoqing.

Chinese public relations at its best. Yu Yan had been given the red-carpet treatment. Due to her pending overseas adoption, she had been singled out as an ambassador of China. She was dressed to convey a level of excellence. Yu Yan looked healthy. My guess was that over the last few months they had fed her better. She was wearing a brand new yellow sundress over a disposable diaper.

Her tiny body wrapped around Mrs. Qiang. Her eyes were still vacant, with no concept of the new world she would enter. My first instinct was to hold my arms out to her. I had spent many hours wondering how this tiny person had survived the harsh winter on the fourth floor with no heating. I'd have to take it slowly. Seven months had passed since my previous visit. That was a long time.

Mrs. Qiang placed Yu Yan into my open arms. Her legs were free of rashes. She smelled clean. No urine odor.

And the child did not resist. She simply bent her legs around my waist and found a new body to take refuge in. Warmth inflated my heart as I pulled Yu Yan close, hoping one day this little girl would learn to laugh and know the love of her new family.

This was the first step toward a new life for our entire family. Having Yu Yan at home began to register. It was happening. I'd be taking her home. Today was the beginning I had waited for.

The official handed me a bill for three hundred US dollars. I nervously took out my traveler's checks. His eyebrows narrowed, "We take cash."

"Where do you expect me to find U.S. cash?"

"You go White Swan Hotel, they change for cash."

Mrs. Qiang motioned to me that she would drive me. Yu Yan sat on my lap remaining quiet.

The White Swan flaunted a four-star rating with all the amenities of a US hotel. It felt refreshing to walk through the doors. The Bank of China was in the lobby.

I handed the lady behind the counter my U.S. travelers' checks.

"We cannot give U.S. dollars."

"But I'm giving you U.S. dollars, why is that a problem?"

Her face did not flinch. "No U.S. dollars."

Having lived in Hong Kong, I knew she couldn't help me.

"Can you call your manager, please?"

A young man in a tailored blue suit and bright red tie approached. "I'm sorry, but I cannot exchange U.S. dollar, but I will give you the equivalent in RMB, the local currency, at a rate of 9 to 1."

I was too tired to argue. I figured the bill would have to be paid in local currency and hoped there would not be a conflict back at the Civil Affairs Department.

I returned to the Civil Affairs Department to settle the bill. The officer did not question my payment in the Chinese currency, RMB. Why he had not told me that was an option would remain a mystery. I didn't know what bill I was paying, but knew better than to ask questions. This would be the first of many bills to come.

Yu Yan and I followed Mrs. Qiang into the car assuming we were heading back to the orphanage. Sign language was our form of communication. An hour into our journey, we pulled up in front of a white concrete building with bright red Chinese characters flashing against the black sky.

We entered the restaurant through two wooden doors and were greeted with bright lights and the standard interior decor of local Chinese restaurants. There were twenty round tables covered with white cotton tablecloths, terrazzo tiled floors and sparsely placed paintings of the Yangtze River on the walls.

I was relieved to see the conservative orders that arrived: fried rice, Chinese noodles with vegetables and roast chicken. Yu Yan's appetite was impressive. Her palate had never experienced the pleasure of such diversity.

It was now 8:45 p.m. and I knew that Miguel was expecting my call. I saw no phone, so I'd have to wait until I got to the hotel.

We arrived at the Overseas Hotel in Zhaoqing at 11:30 p.m. Mrs. Qiang handed Yu Yan to me and said goodnight. Holding Yu Yan in my arms felt comfortable. I was looking forward to spending quality time with her.

I unlocked my room door, put Yu Yan on the bed and reached for the phone. Miguel answered, and I could sense his fury across the ocean.

"Do you have any idea how worried we've been? I've called friends in Hong Kong to try and locate you," he said.

"You have a responsibility to this family, you have two children here, and there is no excuse for not contacting us."

I sat and listened as he vented for two more minutes. I knew I deserved the onslaught. There was no rebuttal. I didn't respond as I realized it would've been futile.

CHAPTER 14

THE PROCESS OF PATIENCE

Yu Yan had remained silent. During dinner, she diligently ate her food. Her movements were precise, and she consumed every grain of rice on her plate. On the drive to the hotel, she sat on my lap; no smiles, no grimaces - stoic, emotionless. I tried to step into her shoes, to imagine the journey she was undertaking. Here she was, sitting on a bed, with a woman she barely knew. She showed no signs of fear, or, for that matter, joy. Her hair was in the spike mode- small tufts of black hair standing at attention. She could have been mistaken for a boy.

I wanted to find a way to bond with her. I remembered a conversation with my Aunt Gail, who was a social worker in Canada.

"Lee, you need to be realistic. Adopting a child at the age of three is risky."

"I am realistic. I know it'll take a while for us to connect, but in a loving environment she will begin to learn and grow."

Aunt Gail was trying to make a point.

"A mother and child bond immediately after birth and during the months that follow. It's highly unlikely that you and Yu Yan will ever connect on that level."

I could feel my defenses standing guard. "We may not bond as quickly as a biological child, but I promise you we'll connect. Either way, I can offer her a future."

The following morning was Friday, July 8. I called the Chinese Translators Society to see if Erin was working. Luckily for me she was. She re-arranged her schedule to accommodate me, for which I was eternally grateful.

I was embarking on the Chinese side of the adoption. All of the U.S. related paperwork and application had been approved. The next few days would be spent gathering documents to allow Yu Yan to come to the US. I knew my tolerance would be tested working with local officials.

We collected Ms. Qiang from the orphanage and left Yu Yan to play with her peers.

The three of us walked to the Notary Department where we met two young Chinese women. I would be collecting the Chinese documentation which was information regarding Yu Yan. They took us into a room with red clay floors and three cherry wood benches. A woman asked me to take a seat and then to answer questions regarding my family background. The process took two hours.

She showed me all the documents related to the adoption from the Chinese government: an Abandonment Letter, a Letter Authorizing the Adoption, and a Chinese Medical Report. I asked for five copies. The lady told me that all the paperwork needed to be notarized and would be ready for collection at four. It was Friday and the government offices would be closed over the weekend.

Erin turned to me and said, "I go now. I meet you Monday at nine. We have lots of work to do."

I embraced and thanked her.

I went to collect Yu Yan from the orphanage. She was playing quietly in the nursery. I gathered her into my arms, and she let out an ear shattering cry. I stood stunned but amused to see that she was capable of emotion. We made our exit, her shrill screams echoing off the walls.

Being a foreigner, onlookers turned to watch me carrying a hysterical Chinese child in my arms. When I reached the sidewalk, a pathway through the crowds naturally carved away. Pedestrians stopped and stared. Eventually I put Yu Yan on the ground and let her walk. I slowed my pace to match her tiny steps. The locals looked on dumbfounded, staring unabashedly as we made our way to the hotel. No one intervened.

On Saturday morning, we had lots of hours to fill. Yu Yan and I wandered into the restaurant. Her walking had improved. A buffet consisted of rice congee, Singapore noodles, white bread, sponge cake spirals, hard rolls, egg sandwiches and fresh eggs prepared to order. I opted for two slices of toast and got Yu Yan the rice congee. I thought it best to slowly introduce her to different foods. I sat her in front of me and tapped her hand to get her attention. She raised her eyes and met mine.

I pointed to myself. "Mum." I touched her chest. "Zhoe." I could've been conversing with a stuffed doll. Her blank stare showed no acknowledgement.

After breakfast, Yu Yan and I gathered a stack of coloring books and crayons that I'd brought with me and walked to the orphanage.

We climbed the concrete steps to the fourth floor, the familiar stench of urine welcoming us. The children were in their summer wear of simple shorts, tops and bare feet. The nursery was empty. It was the first time I'd witnessed that. My mind flashed back to my first visit when I had seen the baby in the dying room. I still wondered if others had met the same fate.

The children were cheerful and receptive to the coloring books. While they busied themselves with their new pictures, I walked through each of the rooms. I heard a whimper in the nursery but knew it wasn't possible because there were no babies. I stepped into the Dying Room and felt relieved to find it empty. I saw a small cardboard box the size of a computer on the far table.

I sat beside one of the children and helped her color. I stopped and listened intently for a few seconds. I heard the whimper again. I walked back into the Dying Room. My eyes remained on the cardboard box. A roach scurried over the edge. I became transfixed. I felt the goose bumps rising. I couldn't swallow.

I waited another ten seconds and clearly heard a moan coming from the box. My feet felt like cement blocks as I made my way to the far corner. I reminded myself to breathe. The dampness of the room enveloped me. The box was now in front of me. My hand shook. I pulled open the flap and my fear was confirmed. A baby! She was tiny and ashen white. All life draining from her as she gasped for her last breath. Two roaches scuttled over her body.

A worker walked in. She nonchalantly picked up the baby's fingers and let her arm flop back down, then she signaled with her own hands, "Baby, too small. No good no more." Her icy stare met my eyes as I fought to stop the tears.

I was helpless. I remembered Mick Marshall's words, "Lee, help the ones you can, and walk away from the ones you can't." How was it possible that the workers became indifferent to a suffering child? I reminded myself, this is a different culture. I pitied them, for they knew no better. The worker motioned for me to leave, and I did. I prayed the baby's last breath would be fast.

The workers had decided the fate of this baby. And like countless other human lives, this one did not warrant priority. I remembered reading that people who die, are lucky, for they are going to paradise. It is those who remain alive that live to suffer. I hoped this little girl's journey would be swift.

We stayed until after lunch, and I observed Yu Yan playing with her peers. I watched as she returned her chair to its appropriate place on the far wall.

When I went to collect Yu Yan to leave, a worker held her and she had no intention of coming with me. I pulled her out of the worker's arms, at which point she screamed. The outburst caught me off guard. I had hoped after two nights in a comfy bed with good food there would've been a connection. The dire conditions at the orphanage were still more enticing for her, than coming with me.

I made my exit hastily and clambered down the four flights of stairs unto the crowded street. Yu Yan cried for the next four hundred yards. We passed a construction site and a loud drilling noise pierced the air. Like a flipped switch, Yu Yan immediately stopped crying. I think the sound scared her.

Once in the hotel room, I undressed her tiny body. Like a doll, she stood virtually lifeless, no cooperation, no expression. I turned the bath tap on and let the warm water rise until the tub filled a third of the way. I poured two caps of rose scented bubble bath under the running water and allowed bubbles to multiply and create a layer of froth for Yu Yan to step into. She didn't attempt to climb in. I lifted her frail body and sat her in the midst of the sudsy water. She showed no excitement or desire to play with the bubbles.

Several minutes later, I dried her and tickled under her arms. Her blank eyes did not flicker, and she had no reaction. I then tried pinching the bottoms of her feet. I wondered if she would flinch or push me away. She did nothing. I left her sitting on the bed when I went for powder. Her back was toward me as I rounded the corner. I crept quietly behind her and yelled, "Boo!" Still, no reaction. I knew that she couldn't be deaf, because she reacted to the drill on the street-or so I thought. She seemed to be a complex little girl.

I heard a soft tapping on the door. I turned the knob and peeked out to see the doctor standing in the hallway with her husband. I welcomed them in and they walked in and sat down. The doctor had brought medicine for Yu Yan. She said that part of the reason for Yu Yan's bloated stomach was worms. They stayed for ten minutes. It was awkward as we spoke through sign language. I gestured my appreciation and they departed.

I tucked Yu Yan under the covers and then slipped under the sheets in the other bed. The nights dragged. This was my third sleep and insomnia had taken over due to a combination of jet lag mixed with anxiety. The black skies seemed infinite.

I picked up the phone and dialed home. Florida was twelve hours behind China. It would be 10:30 on Saturday morning there.

"Hello." The familiar voice of my mum answered.

The static on the phone magnified the distance.

"Hi mum. Sleep isn't cooperating. I thought a conversation with home would help."

"You called at a good time, the girls are in the backyard and Miguel is reading the newspaper."

"Hi mum, are you coming home?" Sierra's sweet voice came on the phone.

"Soon, my love, soon. I miss you lots and lots. I need a few more papers for Zhoe, and then we'll be home."

"Can I talk to her?"

"It's night-night time here. She's fast asleep. Remember, she doesn't speak. You'll have to teach her."

"OK, mum, I'll be a good teacher."

I could hear Havana in the background. "Mummmm."

"Hi, my little love, it's mum. I miss you. I'm coming home soon."

"Bye, Bye."

"That's the best you'll get from her. The girls are filling up the plastic pool with water." Miguel had picked up the phone.

"That's fine, I wanted to hear their voices."

"How's it going?"

I could tell homesickness was creeping in. "Good. Slow. The language barrier is tough. Poor Erin is doing her fair share of work. I just have to be patient. I'm ready to come home."

Miguel's voice was calming. "You're on the homestretch. You'll be running the beach before you know it. You've done great. Love you lots."

"Love you too." I turned over and envisioned hugging each one of them.

Sunday was a quiet day. Yu Yan awoke with a slight fever. I decided to stay in the hotel. In the back of the hotel was a small gazebo with lily ponds and small bridges. I took Yu Yan for a walk. She wandered along slowly, her steps short and indecisive. She stopped and hung her tiny limbs over the bridge and gazed into the small pond below. I longed to know what was going through her mind.

Monday morning arrived and Erin and Ms. Qiang met Yu Yan and me at nine o' clock. We took a taxi to the local police station where the officer handed me a form to fill out details on Yu Yan's background.

There was little information to provide. Sometimes when children are abandoned, a note is left, giving a history. Yu Yan was found in a basket outside of the orphanage door one morning without anything. Even her age remained a mystery. The workers estimated she was seven months old when she was found.

Ms. Qiang took the documents back to the orphanage to fill out. This was the beginning of applying for Yu Yan's passport and exit visa. Once the paperwork was completed, Ms. Qiang would take it to the Foreign Affairs Department for processing. We were told we'd have the travel documents in a few days.

On Tuesday, Yu Yan and I had our morning intake of toast and rice congee. I decided to take her out for a stroll. Her fever had subsided and she seemed in brighter spirits.

Outside the hotel we walked to a park that offered a variety of children's rides. Yu Yan did not crack a smile, but her eyes danced with excitement. The slight show of emotion told me that a small crack in her façade was starting to open. She went on a merry-go-round, an airplane and a few other rides. The rides cost the equivalent of twenty cents each. We stayed for an hour.

We returned to the hotel and ate in the food court, feasting on soup and fried rice, and stayed at the hotel in the afternoon. The phone rang at four fifteen.

Erin's soft voice was on the other end. "Miss Lee, Ms. Qiang say documents ready soon. She call Wednesday."

On Wednesday morning, I was filled with the hope of departing Zhaoqing. Erin called at nine thirty. "Miss Lee, so sorry. Ms. Qiang say Foreign Affairs Department close for study."

Here we go. The waiting game continued. "Erin, can't we speak to someone? Did she not know this yesterday?"

"I no sure. I busy this morning. If you want, I meet you later and we try find someone to talk to.

She was incredible. "Thanks, I'd like that."

I left Yu Yan at the orphanage, having no idea how long the ordeal at the Foreign Affairs department would take. The infamous Chinese waiting game was now in effect.

Erin and I arrived at the Foreign Affairs building, but the doors were locked and we were not allowed to walk into the complex. We went next door to an office that was marked Foreign Marriages. The lady behind the desk allowed us to use her phone. Erin called Foreign Affairs and was told that workers were studying, and she couldn't speak to the director. They were aware of the case and would address it within the next few days.

I felt an adrenaline rush. I refused to accept the vague response. I needed a more definitive answer. A surge of stubbornness engulfed me. Mick had urged me to hold my ground and be forceful because the city offices were known for their delays. I was putting Erin in a predicament. She would usually abide by the laws and be patient.

She sensed my frustration and went far beyond what was expected. Erin spoke to the woman in the Foreign Marriages office. We were told that we could use her back door, which connected into the complex. We were going to try and locate the director of Foreign Affairs.

Erin and I entered a concrete courtyard with classrooms surrounding the square center. We approached two men to ask if they could tell us where to find the director. They gave us a perplexed look and moved on.

We walked around and arrived at a small entrance room. One man sat behind the wooden counter, and another smoked a cigarette on the bench in the room. Erin explained our situation, and they exchanged phrases. After much deliberation and pressure, the man behind the counter dialed a number and handed the phone to Erin. The director was on the phone and told Erin to return tomorrow after lunch and the package would be complete.

Helplessness crept in because I couldn't communicate the urgency of my situation properly. I had to assume that Erin was relaying the correct messages. Erin was pushing herself hard, and I wished that I could've helped in some way.

I collected Yu Yan and walked with Erin back to her office. She turned to me before stepping into the building. "We meet early, 9 a.m."

"Yes. Thanks." I replied

I needed Yu Yan's passport completed by Thursday. I wanted to travel to Guangzhou on Friday to meet with the American Consulate. If not, I'd have to spend the weekend in Guangzhou. Looming in the back of my mind was my scheduled departure date out of Hong Kong on July 19, Tuesday. My flight was booked on frequent-flyer points and would be difficult to change.

Erin and I arrived on Thursday at 9:00 a.m. at the Ministry of Foreign Affairs and asked to see the director. Mick had told me that he had been able to expedite passports in one day. I had to be persuasive. We were shown into a small room behind the entryway.

We shook hands with the director and took a seat on two wooden chairs that were placed in front of his desk. Erin and the director spoke in Mandarin. She translated for me. "He say passport take three days. He try hurry for you. Will do by tomorrow."

"Erin, I know they can do this today. It's simply a matter of him deciding to push it through. Please tell him I need it today."

Erin's eyes darted, her nervousness beginning to show. I wished that I could've taken matters into my own hands, because I could feel Erin's discomfort and knew she was risking causing this man to lose face. He was a senior official, and her role should've been to be more submissive.

The director had his hands clasped across his chest. His eyes remained on me as he listened to Erin. He waited, then got out of his chair and walked into the next room.

I turned to Erin. "I'm sorry I'm putting you in a difficult situation. I know they can issue the passport now, and I'd like to book the train to Guangzhou today."

She patted my arm. "I know. I try. We wait and see."

The director returned and sat in his chair.

"Passport ready at two-thirty." He said.

I saw a smile of satisfaction cross Erin's face.

My mind did the time calculation. The last train to Guangzhou would leave at two. I decided to push my luck.

"Erin, can you tell him that I have a train to catch and need it done by this morning?"

The color drained from Erin's cheeks. I knew I was being brazen, but at this point I was willing to try anything. Erin apprehensively repeated my words.

He looked at me and answered.

Erin translated. "He say it impossible, but promise at two-thirty."

I felt deflated, but knew I had pushed Erin way past her comfort zone.

As we walked out, Erin said, "Go back hotel and wait."

Yu Yan and I returned to the hotel and turned on the television. It was nine forty-five. At five past eleven there was a knock on the door. It was Erin.

A big grin swept over her face. "The director called me. Passport ready. First we go police station collect form.

We need rush back to Ministry of Foreign Affairs before they close at eleven thirty."

I threw my arms around her neck in gratitude, picked up Yu Yan, and we rushed over to the police station to collect the police clearance.

We arrived at the Ministry of Foreign Affairs at eleven twenty-eight and flew into the office. The director handed me Yu Yan's passport. I thanked him in my broken Mandarin and bowed in gratitude. I wanted to hug him.

I invited Erin and Ms. Qiang to lunch at the hotel. This would be my final Chinese banquet for a long time. We took photographs outside, and I said my farewell to Ms. Qiang and the Chinese Overseas Hotel.

Erin went with me to the train station which I appreciated as I was lugging my duffel bag strapped to a pulley behind me and holding Yu Yan in the other arm. On the platform, I turned to her. I felt my emotions rising.

I held her two hands in mine. "A thousand thank-yous would not be enough. Your help this week will be remembered. You were my special angel. Thank you."

She blushed and looked down at her feet. "You good person. We write, OK?"

The tears trickled down my cheeks as I scribbled down my address and took hers. I hugged her tightly and boarded the train with my new daughter.

CHAPTER 15

GUANGZHOU – DAY NINE

We boarded the train and Yu Yan sat beside me. The first phase was complete, two more stages to go. We arrived at Guangzhou at five thirty. Carrying Yu Yan in one arm and dragging my duffel bag behind, I made my way to the taxi stand. A cab arrived, and we headed towards the White Swan Hotel. Entering the lobby, I felt like I'd walked into an oasis. I heard English being spoken and the air conditioner was pumping cool air. I glimpsed the end of the journey.

I had yet to receive a smile from Yu Yan, she did not utter a sound on the train ride. She simply observed and let the scenery soak in. Her world on the fourth floor of the orphanage was fading behind her and a new world was opening before her eyes.

That night I wanted to celebrate. At dinner we sat at a linen-covered table and I ordered from a menu in English. I smiled at the Chinese waiter in his pleated black pants, starched white shirt and red bow tie. "I'd like to order the chicken in mushroom sauce and fried rice for my daughter." I loved saying, "my daughter."

The next morning we went to the American Consulate where clerks gave us a list of items that Yu Yan needed for her interview to qualify for a visa. The interview was scheduled for later the same day.

The first item on the list was a medical exam for Yu Yan. A smiling secretary gave me directions to a nearby clinic.

The whole process was a formality. A nurse in white scrubs recorded Yu Yan's height, weight and used a rubber hammer to check the reflex in her knees. After the final tests, an aide issued me the required medical certificate.

Back at the hotel, I dressed Yu Yan in a red, white and blue dress. With all our forms intact, I was confident. I'd be able to speak for myself for a change and felt somewhat in control. Having dealt with Chinese officials over the last eight days, I looked forward to speaking English with the American officials.

At the Consulate, I entered a room with a row of six officials sitting behind a counter in cubicles separated by Plexiglas. An officer called me over to a booth and I slid my papers through a hole in the Plexiglas. I sat down again and held Yu Yan in my lap. I watched as one officer took my papers and reviewed them. He beckoned another officer over and they conversed.

My heart started to flutter. What could possibly be wrong? I wondered.

The officer leaned towards the cutout in the Plexiglas and spoke to me. "Are you an American citizen?"

"No, but I included in the package a power of attorney from my husband. We've been married for seven years. I'm a green-card holder. My other two daughters are citizens."

He looked over at me. "The law states that the American citizen is the one that is to collect the adopted child."

My mind raced. I thought I was on the home stretch. Now, American officials were creating a problem. It took every ounce of composure that I could muster to speak calmly.

"I've just spent the last eight days negotiating with Chinese officials to get my daughter out of China. This is my last step. Surely you're not going to create more barriers. The power of attorney allows me to take my daughter home."

The official raised his hand. "Let me see what I can do." He left and conversed with another official and then returned. "We will issue the visa. It'll be ready in twenty minutes."

I signed deeply, "Thank you so much."

The official beckoned me over with Yu Yan's visa in his hand. "What flight are you leaving on out of Guangzhou?"

"I fly out of Hong Kong on Tuesday." I replied

He sat down behind the Plexiglas, his forehead wrinkled with concern. "I assumed you were going directly to the United States from here, you'll have difficulty going through Hong Kong because she doesn't have a visa."

I wouldn't be deterred I said, "Well, I'll apply for one."

"It's not that easy. As I see it, you have two options. The most secure one is to take the train towards the border, and disembark at the stop before the border. There is a fifteen-minute walk across the border. At the crossover there is a visa office where you can apply. Your other option is to take a chance with the immigration officers once you leave the train in Hong Kong."

I visualized walking fifteen minutes in the humidity, Yu Yan in one arm, dragging the duffel bag in the other. "Thanks for your suggestions. I think I'll take my chances with the Hong Kong officers."

He shrugged his shoulders. "The best of luck to you."

I reasoned that once I was on Hong Kong soil I could persuade them to let me stay. I'd let the tears fall if need be, whatever it would take to convince them. We returned to the hotel and packed.

We woke early on Saturday morning, ate breakfast and then checked out. I was worried how I'd juggle Yu Yan and the bags to the train station. I asked the clerk to call a taxi to the train station when a Japanese gentleman beside me intervened.

"Excuse me, but I overheard your request. I'll be going to the train station and am going to Hong Kong also. I'd be happy to share a taxi with you."

I smiled gratefully, "Thank you."

He shook my hand and then bowed. "My name is Odo."

He was a wonderful gentleman and helped me with my bag.

We sat together on the three-hour ride to Hong Kong.

"Do you live in Hong Kong?" I asked

"No, I live in the United States I had business in China. Who's the little princess sitting beside you?"

I pulled Yu Yan onto my lap. "This is Yu Yan. She'll be coming home with me for the first time. I have two other toddler daughters at home in Florida."

He had a camera in his bag. "Do you mind if I take a photograph of her? I paint for a hobby."

"No, that's fine."

He clicked the camera a few times and then looked up at me. "I have two daughters in college. I remember when they were her size. The time goes by fast."

The conversation continued to flow for the entire journey. Yu Yan gazed out the window as the life she once knew was passed by.

We pulled into the train station and my nerves were on high alert. I turned to Odo to say good-bye. "Thank you for your company on the ride. I really enjoyed our conversation. It's the first one I've had in ten days."

He bowed. "Likewise. You take care of those three little princesses. They'll be in college before you blink."

I stood in line at the immigration counter and inhaled deeply, conjuring up a tale for my Hong Kong official. I approached the officer with the brightest smile I could muster.

He looked down at the passports and his eyes flashed between Yu Yan and me. One word came from his mouth.

"Visa?"

It was time to tell my tale. "I've just completed the adoption process in China and will be in transit for three days in Hong Kong. Here are our two tickets showing our departure date."

My throat was dry. I waited for what seemed like five minutes as he checked all the documentation. He had yet to make a comment. Carefully and diligently he read all the material in front of him. He stamped our passports. "I'm giving you four days in Hong Kong."

I wanted to jump over the counter and hug him. Instead I said, "Sir, that's all the time we'll need. Thank you so much."

I flew out of the station, thanking the lucky star that now seemed to be following me.

We arrived via taxi at Richard and Nancy Ross's apartment looking like wayward travelers; our hair in a mess with the Chinese dirt covering the pores on our skin. I was grateful that they'd opened up their home to us.

Nancy greeted us at the door. "Come in, come in. You must be exhausted."

We embraced and then I walked over to Mr. Ross. (I couldn't call him Richard. He'd always be *Mr.* Ross). His wide grin was welcoming. He hugged me tightly and gestured towards a chair. "Sit down and tell me details."

Nancy scooped up Yu Yan who had remained standing in the doorway. She sat on Nancy's lap for a few minutes then slid off and stood beside me.

Nancy looked at me. "I'm happy for you, she's finally here."

"The hardest part was the seven months of not knowing when the process would be finalized," I said.

Yu Yan remained silent. Her little mind must have been spinning. While the three of us talked Yu Yan walked away and stood in front of the side table in the living room with her back to me. At first I thought she was looking at something on the table, but she remained motionless for five minutes.

We finished on our conversation and then I called over to her, "Yu Yan, are you OK?" Of course, there was no response. I got up and walked over. I knelt beside her and then realized her eyes were closed. She had fallen asleep standing up.

On Sunday we woke early and had a simple breakfast of toast and juice. Nancy and Mr. Ross spent their Sundays at The American Club. They gave me a temporary card and told me they'd be at the club until the afternoon.

"Nancy and I will be sitting by the pool." Mr. Ross said. "I'm sure you've lots of catching up to do. Check in with us a little before four."

Yu Yan and I walked into the Fireside Lounge that was adjacent to the lobby. Jenny was sitting in there with her husband Bruce and a mutual friend Marc.

Marc was one of Miguel's tennis partners when we lived in Hong Kong. He saw me first. With a surprised look on his face he got up and walked towards me.

"Lee, are you OK? Miguel called us last week. He was really worried." He put his arms around me and squeezed tightly.

Jenny turned around and ran towards me. "Oh my God Lee, I can't believe it's you. Look at her, she's adorable." She lifted Yu Yan into her arms. I followed her back to the couch.

"I'm sorry guys. I had no idea Miguel called you all. It was a crazy week and we lost communication for a few hours on my first day."

Bruce smiled and kissed me on both cheeks. "You look fine to me. Miguel described you as lost and hysterical."

I laughed. "Wow, now that's a little dramatic. Sure didn't paint a pretty picture, did he? I was more out of touch than lost. I didn't have access to a phone and was in a car driving across China."

Marc sat back down. "I guess he had good reason to panic. He's far away and has no control. Anyway, you're here now, and it looks like you survived the ordeal. How does a Mimosa sound?"

"Now, that sounds perfect."

CHAPTER 16

HOME

I boarded the United Airlines Boeing 747 knowing that it would be a long time before my shoes touched Asian soil again.

I had requested bulkhead seats so that Zhoe (from here on, I'd call her by her American name) would be able to move around. She remained silent throughout the morning. Her world had previously consisted of one room. In the past ten days, she had traveled by car, train, subway, ferry and airplane. She had consumed a diversity of foods, eating the smallest crumb no matter what the dish. I still couldn't raise a smile from her. I tried tickling with fingers, feathers, making funny faces, all in vain. I ran out of tactics.

Seated beside us was a gentleman in his late fifties. His friendly blue eyes danced when he spoke. He exuded a calming presence. Dressed in blue jeans, with a camel-colored jacket, he looked comfortable and confident with himself. He extended his hand to me.

"Gordon Jones. Nice to meet you. We might as well get comfy. We've got sixteen hours to entertain ourselves."

"Lee. This is Zhoe. I hope she doesn't bother you."

His eyes rested on Zhoe sitting quietly in her seat.

"Doesn't look like the bothersome sort."

Gordon and I talked for hours. We discussed a diverse range of topics from New Age religion, to death, to politics, to fate and destiny. Conversation put a big dent in the duration of the tedious flight.

All this time Zhoe remained in her own world, not uttering a sound. She sat on the carpeted floor in front of my seat, legs crossed with her eyes empty of all emotion.

When Gordon and I stopped talking. I laid my head against the seat back. This was the first time in two weeks that I could reflect and contemplate the magnitude of events that had taken place in both of our lives. My mind drifted to the Chinese stories I'd read. What it would take for a mother to abandon her child.

In Zhoe's case, I envisioned there was a young Chinese mother who was living with her mother-in-law somewhere in the countryside. She carried a child for nine months, feeling a miracle growing inside of her. A healthy child would be taken for granted. The bloodline had to be carried on by a male.

The first pangs are felt as the pressure increases within her abdomen. The young mother pushes to bring a new life into the world. A little tuft of black hair begins to emerge and the perfect little body was pulled into this man made world from the security of the womb. The bond was instantly ignited between mother and child, once connected from the inside, now they strengthen that bond on the outside. She is placed on the mother's breast and suckles the formula that nature provided. The mother and child are united and remain together for six months. The child absorbs the mother's scent, her voice, her touch- all creating comfort and a lifetime bond.

The decision was obviously not instantaneous for Zhoe's mother. The workers estimated her age to be six months old when dropped off on the orphanage steps. How long did the young woman struggle with her decision? What made her concede to the pressure from her family? At least she gave her baby daughter a chance at survival by bringing her to the orphanage.

I looked down at Zhoe, wishing I could find a way to reach out and let her understand that fate brought us together and we'd have a lifetime of love and happiness. It would take time, but I also knew I had been blessed.

Zhoe's name on her passport read, Guo Yu Yan. Guo was her last name. It was given to all the children in the orphanage, and meant child of the land. Miguel and I decided to rename her Zhoe Guo Solaun.

My daughter remained the perfect traveler. She ate when the food came, slept when tired and sat quietly. I thought she must be experiencing a level of shock and didn't know how to digest the changes happening around her. The scenery, the people, the voices were a new stimulus.

I heard the wheels screech as they touched the tarmac. I turned to Gordon. "Nice meeting you. Thanks for the conversation."

"Mutual, my dear. I wish you all the best with your little gem."

We landed in Los Angeles, where we were to hand in Zhoe's documents. It was the first process in applying for her green card.

The United Airline desk attendant greeted me. "Good morning. Hope you had a nice flight."

I smiled, thankful to be back on western soil. We went on through Atlanta and then to Jacksonville.

The flatness of Florida came into focus beneath the plane. I heard the wheels lower and the voice of the captain tell us, "Please prepare for landing." I felt a wave of relief. Our ordeal was truly over.

My new daughter and I stepped into the waiting lounge. Miguel and my other girls were standing by the walkway. Havana was in Miguel's arms. Her unruly blonde curls fell where they may, her eyes twinkled with curiosity. Sierra was holding Miguel's hand, her thick brown hair pulled back in a ponytail, allowing her piercing black eyes to shine through her bronzed skin.

I walked toward them with Zhoe clinging to me. I could sense a little confusion. I knelt down in front of Sierra and pulled her close to me.

"Sierra, this is your sister Zhoe."

A small smile crossed Sierra's face, and I hugged her again. I stood in front of Miguel and Havana, embracing them both at the same time. Havana seemed a little unsure so I didn't overdo the introduction. Zhoe was motionless. We would have to take it slowly.

All three girls sat in the middle row of our white Chevrolet Lumina van - the family mobile of the nineties. Miguel and I had lots of catching up to do. We let the girls figure out the next step.

The girls took Zhoe under their wings - they held her hand and took her with them. The nights were rough for Zhoe. We would find her curled up on the floor in the living room in the morning. We didn't know if she was sleep-walking or waking up and wandering around.

She was frightened of Miguel and my father, which could be understandable given the fact that she had not been around many men. Whenever Miguel or my father approached, she cried hysterically. This lasted three weeks.

The whole family took her to the beach, horseback riding, playgrounds and the pool. Daily, I saw changes in her physical abilities. She had not mastered the art of running yet, but broke into a fast soldier walk when the other girls ran.

I saw her first sign of a smile a week after she arrived. The girls and I were in the back garden and had filled up a plastic pool that my girls loved to play in. Zhoe was sitting on the grass and the other two girls were splashing water at her. Her lips closed and a ghost of a smile emerged.

I took Zhoe for her first American physical and inoculations. Her stool tests were sent to Washington because they discovered a parasite that they couldn't identify. It was still too early to detect deformities and handicaps but the doctor thought it highly unlikely that she had either.

At two-and-a-half years old she weighed nineteen pounds and was half-inch shorter than Havana who was seventeen months old.

Remembering Maria Montessori's philosophy on education in allowing children to progress at their own speed and allowing integration of different ages. I knew Sierra and Havana would be good role models.   Even though no words were spoken, by observing the other girl's actions, Zhoe progressed quickly.

Zhoe watched the girls interact with me, saw them break into giggles, saw them share toys, and love one another. I stayed on the outskirts and watched the phenomena unfold. Within weeks, Zhoe was laughing and ready to attempt activities that came her way.   Her progression became rapid and constant.   She began by saying one word, than a sentence and within six months conversations began.

During dinner it was a treat to watch Zhoe eat.   She chewed each bite twenty-five times and not a grain of rice could be found on her plate when she finished eating. One night I was washing the dishes while she ate a chicken meal.   I walked over to the table and saw her chewing the drumstick.   I realized she had never seen bones before.   She had been taught to eat the last scrap of food in her bowl.

I kept her at home with Havana while Sierra attended pre-school.   We discovered the art of tracing letters.   In the mornings I would have the two of them sit at the kitchen table and work on one page of letters.   Havana would be finished after one page.   Zhoe sat and did eight more.

A year later, when Zhoe was three, my sister Ann and her family visited from Canada for the summer.   Ann was pregnant with her fourth child.   The girls' curiosity was piqued when they saw their aunt's protruding stomach.   Sierra was the first to react.

"Auntie Ann, why's your stomach fat?"   Sierra asked.

That began a string of questions that brought forth a discussion on biological and adopted children. Ann, being a teacher was familiar with these conversations. She knew to just answer what was asked and not expound on more that was needed.

"I have a baby in my tummy." Ann answered.

Sierra's eyes widened, and Havana and Zhoe were now intrigued.

Sierra turned to me. "Mummy, was I in your tummy?"

"Yes," I answered, my nerves a little on edge as I saw the pattern evolving.

Havana then said, "Mummy, was I in your tummy?"

"Yes," I said, taking a deep breath and waiting patiently for the third question.

On cue, Zhoe looked at me and asked, "Mummy, was I in your tummy?"

I sat down on the couch and pulled Zhoe onto my lap. With my arm around her waist, I repeated her tale. "Remember the story I told you about China. You were in the tummy of a woman who lived in China. When I visited China, I saw you and fell in love with you and was lucky when I got to bring you home and become your mum."

Her charcoal eyes looked directly into mine. "I have another mum?"

"Yes." I then waited for the next question. It didn't come.

Unbothered, she jumped off my lap and went to play outside.

Not another word was spoken about her birth until two years later.

We were living in Singapore Zhoe, was five. Zhoe and I stepped in the elevator going to our apartment on the seventh level. We were both leaning against the back wall looking at the numbered lights blink as we passed each floor, lost in our own worlds. Suddenly she looked up at me and asked,

"Mum, if I have another mother, then I must have another father?"

I was caught off guard that it took me a second to respond. "Yes, you do."

The doors opened, she walked off and didn't ask another question.

Through the years, Zhoe expressed minimal interest in her life before our family. I assembled a photo album of her time in the orphanage, but questions were rare.

She survived the orphanage due to her ability to block out the surroundings. In our family she was safe and happy. I think she wanted to be a part of Sierra and Havana's world. In order for her to do that, China could not have a role in her new life. With time, the little memory she had of the orphanage was erased and her American lifestyle became her.

I ask myself, now, twenty-years later as a wiser and well-traveled woman, would I undertake the challenge of adopting a child from China? With the factual evidence on Zhoe's medical conditions, would I be brave enough now to embrace the task? Now I'd analyze the details and weigh all the pros and cons. The practical side of my brain would take over and the decision to adopt a handicapped child deemed more difficult.

With age, fear inhibits action.

Looking back at the unwavering twenty-seven-year-old woman who was driven to make a difference, I could see that naïve idealism pushed her forward to change the lives of those less fortunate. Like a racehorse, she put on blinders keeping the finish line in focus. A Chinese law that prohibited couples under the age of thirty-five did not deter her. A medical diagnosis of serious handicaps did not sway her decision. Learning to overstep her comfort zone with Chinese Officials fueled her determination. How I envy the fearlessness of my youth, the advantages of being naïve and idealistic.

I embarked on a journey to change the lives of Chinese orphans, but in truth, the abandoned children of Zhaoqing, taught me more life lessons than any classroom.   I heard laughter shared amongst those living in squalor. Their innate happiness of children was genuine.   I saw them embrace strangers unconditionally, never judging or criticizing.   I witnessed a roomful of orphans show appreciation for the meager bowls of food placed in front of them. I was humbled by those half my age and my life changed forever.

My life was touched most by the child that didn't speak a word.   Zhoe at the age of two had overcome more hardship than I had at the age of twenty-seven.   At two, she had found a way to survive the harshest conditions life had dealt her. Her deep dark eyes reached out to me and spoke of her inner strength. The bond formed instantly. She dared me to defy obstacles that prohibited our becoming family. She pushed me far beyond what I thought I was capable of. Zhoe empowered me.

Today, Zhoe is a thriving college student. My trio of teenage daughters contributed the grey highlights in my brown hair evenly.   I'd ask the girls if they sat up at night and conspired who'd hold the baton in the relay race to "drive mum insane". Along the way Zhoe mastered the game of tennis and played competitively as a junior. As a sophomore in high school she enrolled in the Rotary Exchange program and lived in Argentina for a year. She arrived home fluent in Spanish.

Zhoe, is my Chinese pearl, a treasured jewel I was blessed to find.

EPILOGUE

1997 - SINGAPORE – 6 SEPTEMBER

I ran as fast as I could while holding the hands of Sierra and Havana. I was panting by the time I reached the subway security office, a small square counter enclosed with Plexiglas. A male and female officer perched on stools inside. I began to ramble at double-speed with my Jamaican accent.

"My daughter is on the train. Alone. A thousand strangers. She's gone. What am I going to do? Hurry, we need to find her." I was yelling through a small hole the size of an orange.

The officer, looked at me with her round, black button eyes, "Calm down," she said. "You need to give us a description of your daughter. We will radio the next station and have officers go on board and try to locate her. But ma'am, you have to calm down."

"Sorry. She's wearing a pink dress with a white sweater and white sandals. She's six years old. How will you ever find her? The train is packed solid."

"Give us time. We'll do the best that we can."

Sierra and Havana were in shock, their tearful eyes wide, trying to be brave. My mind was frantic with thoughts of what Zhoe must be feeling at this time. She didn't even know our phone number. She must be terrified. My heart beat faster than I could count. I kept reassuring myself: We're living in Singapore, one of the most conscientious countries in the world. It's safe. She'll be OK.

Ten minutes passed, and I turned around and inhaled slowly, trying to keep positive thoughts. I scanned the crowds and glanced over at the up escalator.

My heart jumped as I saw Zhoe's jet-black hair and then her small ivory face. Her eyes were wide with fear, but stoic, not a tear on her cheek. She was holding the hand of a young Chinese business woman. My girls saw her instantly too. My tears flowed as I rushed towards her with open arms.

"Zhoe, I'm so sorry sweetie, are you OK?" I looked up at the young woman, dressed neatly in her blue crisp suit with a black leather briefcase in her hand.

"Thank you, thank you! How can I ever repay you?"

A smile crossed her sweet face, "She's OK. Please, it's OK."

She was standing behind Zhoe on the train and saw what happened. She took Zhoe by the hand, disembarked at the next stop then caught the train back to our station.

I bent down to embrace Zhoe and the young Chinese woman slipped away. Sierra put her small hand on my shoulder. "Mummy, why are you crying? We found her."

My mind flashed back to China to the first time I'd found Zhoe. I pulled all three girls close. "No, my love, this time, Zhoe found us."

Lee and Zhoe in 2013

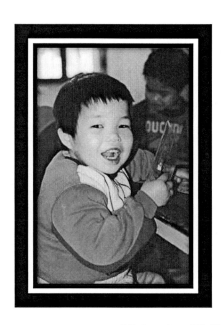
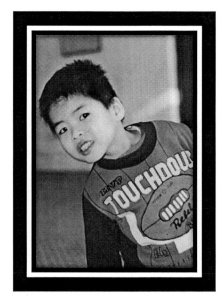

China's Children – Zhaoqing

ACKNOWLEDGEMENTS

I believe in life you surround yourself with friends that contribute to different aspects to your life. A friend to confide in. A friend to go for a run with. A friend in a book club.

A lifetime friendship that began in grade school. A new friend that brightens your day.

In undertaking to publish this book it took the collaboration of family, friends and strangers. Everyone playing an important role in getting *Child of the Land* to print.

I'd like to first thank my parents whose unending support offered me opportunities that created the foundation of the person I am today. My father is my biggest fan and even though a bit biased, his constant words of encouragement and praise allowed me to always dream big.

To my amazing daughters, Sierra, Zhoe and Havana whose input was invaluable. Not, to be forgotten, my youngest, son, Dakota, 8, who kept saying, "Aren't you done with Zhoe? You still have to write about Sierra and Havana. Then it's me, right?"

This manuscript collected dust for over fifteen years. I shared the pages with my high school Commerce teacher, Mr. Terry Cook, a mentor and friend. His loyal support and advice gave me confidence to take the next step from writing to publishing.

I joined a writing pod and my "poddies", Noel, Frances, Jo and Dave gave weeks of constructive critiques that elevated my writing to the next level. Thank you.

A huge thank you to all my friends who took the time to read my book, giving helpful hints and new ideas.

A thank you, to all the talented artists who submitted designs for my cover. None of whom I got to meet, but showed endless enthusiasm and creativity. To Dee, whose patience and artistry created the perfect cover.

Thank you, seems insufficient when everyone's contribution allowed my dream to become a reality, but it's a start, Thank you.